9/92

8

The Taste of
SPAIN

The Taste of SPAIN

Traditional Spanish recipes and their origins

Camilla Jessel

ST. MARTIN'S PRESS, NEW YORK

For Micky and Alfonso,
my best critics

THE TASTE OF SPAIN

THE TASTE OF SPAIN
Text © 1990 by Camilla Jessel

Photography by Manuel Diaz and Francesco Venturi

Landscape photography © 1990 by Francesco Venturi/KEA

For information, address St. Martin's Press, 175 Fifth Avenue,
New York, N.Y. 10010.

ISBN 0-312-06478-0

Library of Congress Cataloging-in-Publication Data
Jessel, Camilla
The taste of Spain   Camilla / Jessel,
p. cm.
ISBN 0-312-06478-0
1. Cookery, Spanish
2. Restaurants, lunch rooms, etc, Spain, Guide-books
3. Spain, Description and travel-1981-Guide-books
I. Title
TX723.5.$047 1991
641.5946-dc20   91-14145 CIP
First published in Great Britain by Tauris Parke Books
First U.S. edition
10 9 8 7 6 5 4 3 2 1
Photosetting by Spire Origination Limited, Norwich
Color separation by Fabbri, Milan, Italy
Printed in Hong Kong

CONTENTS

INTRODUCTION
Page 6

1
TAPAS · SNACKS
Page 16

2
ENTRADAS · FIRST COURSES
Page 36

3
SOPAS · SOUPS
Page 62

4
PESCADOS Y MARISCOS · FISH AND SHELLFISH
Page 80

5
CARNE Y AVES · MEAT AND POULTRY
Page 104

6
POSTRES · DESSERTS
Page 136

INDEX
Page 158

·INTRODUCTION·

When I first came to Spain thirty years ago I may not have known much about the country or about its food, but I was certainly willing to learn. Fortunately, I also possessed the right qualifications – interest and a good appetite. Spaniards love people who enjoy their food and are always willing to tell you all about it. Sometimes it was (and still is) difficult to turn down a second helping for fear of offending. I have never forgotten trying unsuccessfully to refuse more of some little cakes called *mantecados* that (on this occasion) tasted strongly of olive oil! For then, in the sixties, people tended to use too much oil, and the country had a reputation for 'greasy' food. At that time, Spain was still suffering from the after-effects of the Civil War, and under Franco was very cut off from the rest of Europe. But I was lucky enough to have a husband who adored good food and a father-in-law, the Marquis of Acapulco, who was not only a wonderful cook and gourmet, but loved to frequent the best restaurants – where his comments were respected, sometimes feared . . .

So, the willing pupil had a wonderful *maestro* who showed her not only the Madrid restaurants but others such as *Candido* in Segovia, where we ate the baby lamb which is so succulent and tender it can be cut with a plate. He also took me north to San Sebastian, the gastronomic capital of the Basque Country. For me it was all so new and different to sit in the port and eat grilled sardines,

or go to neighbouring towns such as Orio and eat sea bream or an enormous beef chop cooked outdoors on a charcoal grill. Then there were excursions up to remote *caserios*, or farmhouses, to eat *pochas*, a special sort of bean, and quails. In the evening, the restaurants had such a variety of fish it was hard to choose, although we usually went to a place offering a speciality, be it lobster, small squid or hake which the Basques cook to perfection. We used to travel to San Sebastian by car, and there were always special stopping places for lunch. One of them was *Casa Ojeda* in Burgos, where the lamb and *morcilla*, a black blood sausage made in these parts with rice, were exceptional. I don't know how we ever reached our destination without a siesta!

So one could eat well in the sixties if one knew where to go and what to eat, and in fact this has been a guideline for me ever since. I always try to find out about a place before going there and eat

THE DRAMATIC GORGE AT RONDA, IN ANDALUSIA, SPANNED BY THE PUENTE NUEVO.

what's been recommended. Experiments can be disastrous as I learned after a few bad experiences. Once, deciding to be on the safe side in an out-of-the-way place, I thought fried eggs would be the best thing to have, with some delicious bread and wine. To my horror the eggs arrived swimming in oil, so from then on I have always made it clear I wanted them drained!

THE DEVELOPMENT OF SPAIN'S CUISINE

Although things have changed tremendously in Spain since I arrived, I thought it would be interesting to explain a few of the historical, geographical and climatological factors that have influenced eating habits around the country. For Spain has no national cuisine – logically enough, as it once consisted of many individual kingdoms, and it is huge in area – and only a few dishes are truly popular nationwide. If you take a look at the map of Spain, then it is not hard to recognize that a great many people, those who live on or near the coast – whether north, south, east or west – are obviously fish eaters. This explains why, for example, Catalan cooking along the north-east coast bears more resemblance to Valencian cooking to the south than to the Catalan food eaten inland. The food eaten along the north coast on the Bay of Biscay – in Galicia, Asturias and Old Castile – is basically simple, relying on the excellent natural produce available from both land and sea. But if we travel

east along that coast into the Basque Country, we get an entirely different, more sophisticated cuisine which is greatly due to the proximity of France and the rest of Europe. The culinary reputation of this part of the country is also due, however, to the region's renowned *cofradías* or gastronomic societies. There are hundreds of these throughout the region, and they are strictly 'men only' (curious in a strongly matriarchal society, where most of the home cooking is done by the women). These gourmet clubs are altogether classless, and their members use the kitchens, buy food, invite friends and enjoy long and copious meals at which food is the main topic of discussion. Many new creations and chefs have emanated from these *cofradías*.

The centre of Spain is renowned for its roasts – the land here is far from the sea, and dishes of roast lamb, sucking pig and kid have led to it being christened the *Zona de los Asados*. The east coast, from the southern parts of the Levante up to and beyond Valencia, is famed for its rice dishes, not surprisingly as there are many stretches of swampy rice fields. Andalusia in the south is as well known for its fried foods, and these basic generalities are even more marked by history than they are by geography: invasions, occupations and introductions throughout the centuries have had a great effect on eating habits.

The earliest inhabitants of Spain, the Iberians, were followed by the Celts who left their mark on

the north-westernmost region of Spain, Galicia. There you'll find savoury meat and fish pies peculiar to that part of Spain alone. The Phoenicians entered Spain on the southern Mediterranean coast, particularly the small stretch between Cadiz and Gibraltar, with its excellent tunny fishing grounds. There they founded the first fish-processing 'factories'. However, here in Andalusia, the most major influence, and on a much wider scale, came from the Romans. When Scipio's legions invaded Spain, they brought with them three vital products – garlic, wheat and grape vines – and a fourth which was to transform the landscape, the olive tree. This also transformed Andalusian cooking, as animal fat gave way to what is today generally regarded as the healthiest of cooking fats, olive oil. This in turn is almost certainly why frying has become the Andalusian speciality, and why the area is known as *Zona de los Fritos*. (It took a long time, for example, for olive oil to travel to the north of the country, to Galicia, not until about the eighteenth century.)

The major influence on Spain in a lasting sense, however, was that of the Moors, Muslim Arabs from North Africa, who first invaded in AD 711, and were not finally banished from the country until 1492. The Arabs not only introduced new methods of cooking but brought with them spices such as nutmeg, black pepper and saffron, and herbs, vegetables, fruit and nuts, among them citrus such as oranges and lemons, and almonds.

Some of the herbs they introduced were already growing wild in the Andalusian hills – most herbs originate from around the Mediterranean area – but the local people had not thought of using them to flavour food. During those eight centuries, the Arabs introduced sweet and sour combinations, using fruit with savoury meats or fish, or honey in sauces (they also planted sugar cane). The word *adobo*, meaning a marinade, is of Arab origin, as are lots of the honey and almond based sweets such as *turrón* or nougat. These are mainly produced on the east coast where the Arabs found the ideal conditions for planting *ar-rozz* as rice is called in Arabic (*arroz* in Spanish).

The Spaniards themselves played a part in forming Spain's cuisine. From the Middle Ages, nomadic shepherds, who basically lived off lamb, cheese and milk, would move from one region to another, depending on the season, and with them went their cooking pots. They might have gone from León in the north down to Extremadura in the west, or from Extremadura to Valencia in the east; in each area they'd find different produce and into their pots would go different ingredients, all of which would be subjected to long slow cooking resulting in the *cocido* dishes we eat today. Another influence was, as in France, what might be called 'peasant' cuisine. In the farm lands of Extremadura, for instance, rich landowners used to keep the so-called 'good' parts of the pig for themselves, and give the innards and 'inferior' meat

to the workers. As a result, they were obliged to devise ways of cooking these portions of the animal, and thereby made all sorts of delicious sausages, cured meats and sauces. These creations of necessity have lasted and become part of the national cuisine, and this is why Extremadura is famed for many excellent pork dishes. (In fact the pigs bred there are fed on acorns, so the meat and hams are of the best quality.)

Spain's convents and monasteries have also had an influence on Spanish cuisine, being at one time the repositories of the culinary arts. Two of the latter in Extremadura, Alcántara and Yuste, were particularly important. It was to Yuste that the gastronomic Charles V decided to retire after abdicating as Holy Roman Emperor. Judging from some of the wonderful-sounding and extensive menus that still exist, it is not surprising that he died of over-eating; they included dishes such as pheasant and pigeon that had been marinated in port for twenty-four hours and then stuffed with liver and truffles (washed down with swigs of a quarter of a litre of Rhine wine at a time)! A superb recipe book from Alcántara was confiscated by French invaders during the Peninsular War; the great Escoffier was later to remark that this book was the only worthwhile French acquisition of that war. The many custard desserts so characteristic of Spain were due to nuns in convents throughout the vine-growing area of the country; they used the egg yolks given them by wine-makers who needed the whites to clarify the wine.

Yet another influence on Spanish cooking – and indeed on the cooking of Europe – was the voyages of the explorers Pizarro and Cortés (both from Extremadura), and Christopher Columbus, a Genoese Jew who, under the patronage of Ferdinand and Isabella of Spain discovered the New World. When they returned, they brought back to Spain the products which would spread throughout the whole of the Old World – the tomato, sweet pepper, maize, potato, pineapple and chocolate.

The earliest cookery books in fact come from Spain, from Catalonia. Apart from some Arab manuscripts, and a book translated from Catalan into Castilian in 1477 of the recipes of Rubert de Nola, a Catalan chef, the first major work was the *Libre de Sent Sovi*, written in the fourteenth century (some fifty or so years before the great French work, Taillevent's *Viandier*). It is not surprising, therefore, that some experts consider that perhaps the best food in Spain comes from the Ampurdán area of Catalonia, in the extreme north-east of the region. As in the Basque Country, the proximity to France and the rest of Europe is evident, although in different ways. Catalonia had close connections with Italy, for instance, which is perhaps why one can eat excellent *cannelloni* there. The main characteristics of Catalan cuisine, however, are the use of lard and olive oil as fats, sweet and sour combinations, and four basic

sauces. The first of these is *sanfaina*, made from onion, tomato, pepper, courgette and aubergine. *Picada* is made from crushed garlic, parsley, almonds, hazelnuts, pine kernels and breadcrumbs, either fried, toasted or soaked (all mashed to a paste which is then added to whatever it is intended to enrich, a rabbit stew for example). The third sauce, or rather base for a sauce, is the *sofrito*, made by gently sautéing chopped onion, garlic, parsley and a little tomato. Finally, there is *allioli*, made from garlic and olive oil, and which is eaten with grilled meat or fish or, for example, with artichokes. Catalan cooking is as varied as its climate. In the hilly regions of the province of Lérida, sometimes referred to as the 'poor relation of Catalonia' (rather unjustly as it has a cuisine of its own), are produced some of the best sausages in Spain – among them the *fuet* or *salchichon de Vich*, similar to Italian salami. The mountains of La Cerdanya are a paradise for all sorts of mushrooms, game, trout from the streams and, of course, vegetables. Taken as a whole, Catalonia is a region rich in vegetables of all kinds, as well as cereals, fruits, vines, and the wonderful fish and shellfish from the coast.

SPANISH COOKING TODAY

It is interesting to look back and see the changes that began in the seventies. With a move towards decentralisation and the dividing of the country into Autonomous Regions, suddenly there was great competition and a desire to rediscover local culinary specialities and traditions. At that time in the Basque Country, in the steps of Paul Bocuse and his *nouvelle cuisine*, a talented group of young chefs started *La Nueva Cocina Vasca*, the new Basque cuisine. This trend was followed in other parts of the country, although not always so successfully, and in fact now the tendency is towards the traditional but using modernized methods. In Catalonia, more or less the same thing happened. What mattered, however, was the general interest being aroused in food and eating all over the country, something that many tourists all too frequently miss out on, too often going to the 'wrong places'. Now there are plenty of good guide books, and I'd highly recommend *Gourmetour* for anyone coming to Spain, or the *Campsa Guide*. If you are driving through small places, it's better to go to the restaurants someone else has tried first; trial and error are for those with more time to spare.

In this book I have tried to select some of the most representative dishes from different parts of the country which can be made without difficulty in most other countries and which will also appeal to most tastes. Paulino, who has converted his simple restaurant into one of the busiest places in Madrid with his innovations and inexpensive prices, insisted I should include *callos* or tripe, because then people would eat it when they came to Spain, knowing it was one of the specialities. I've

DESERT-LIKE HILLS IN THE ANDALUSIAN INTERIOR.
HERE FORTIFIED WINES ARE MADE AND DRUNK BY
FARMERS IN THE FIELDS WHERE WATER IS SCARCE.

IN THE CENTRE OF SPAIN, IN THE REGION OF NEW
CASTILE, WINDMILLS DOMINATE THE SKYLINE OF THE
TOWN OF CAMPO DE CRIPTANA, BETWEEN ALCÁZAR
AND MOTA.

resisted because it is a dish for strong stomachs, and it took me a long time to get used to it. I began by liking the sauce, then gradually moved on to the tripe that had a meaty, as opposed to spongy, appearance. In the end, I found tripe delicious! Maybe I shouldn't have deprived you . . .

Over the years and living more or less in the same area of Madrid, I've become very fond of many little places that have aided my culinary eduction enormously. It is also nice to see how they have progressed over the years, but not really changed at all. I'll always have good memories of *La Colorada* where the simplest and best quality food was produced out of one of the tiniest kitchens imaginable. *Los Arcos*, although it has enlarged its premises, is still one of the places where true Castilian food is served at very reasonable prices, and I never visit Barcelona without going to *Culleretes*. When I first came to Spain in the sixties all these places existed alongside top restaurants such as *Jockey, Horcher* and *El Bodegon*. There were also marvellous places in the old quarter such as *Casa Paco, El Schotis,* and *Lucio* where your meat was and still is served on a sizzling hot clay plate. *Botin*, where roast lamb and sucking pig are the order of the day, is an historical landmark, as is *L'Hardy* which opened in 1839 and whose customers included kings, queens and politicians. I still, all these years later, excitedly anticipate some new speciality, or simply enjoy the wonderful traditional food, every time I go out for

a meal in Madrid, or anywhere in Spain . . .

THE WINES AND OTHER DRINKS OF SPAIN

Wine is one of Spain's great products, for which we have to thank the Romans. The largest wine-producing area in the country is La Mancha in New Castile, in the centre of the country. The bulk of the wine is made for everyday consumption, and Valdepeñas, bordering on Andalusia, is by far the largest and most famous of the Manchegan demarcated wine regions. Light and fresh in taste, it is the staple house wine of bars and restaurants all over the country. Another region, actually called La Mancha, produces some thirty-five per cent of all Spanish wines, some of the young whites being very pleasant and inexpensive.

For white wines, however, it is Catalonia to my mind that takes the prize, and the Torres family are primarily responsible for this. Not only do they produce nearly every sort of wine you can think of, but they are always experimenting with grapes from abroad; one of their most successful is the *Viña Esmeralda*, for which vines were brought from Alsace. *Cava*, Catalonia's most widely exported sparkling wine, is made by the *méthode champenoise* mainly at San Sadurní de Noya, not far south of Barcelona. It is well worth a visit as nearly every second door seems to be a *bodega*.

For the great reds the Rioja is the place, and as

more and more are now being exported, they are becoming much better known. One of the great *bodegas, El Marqués de Riscal* in Rueda, produces a nice white as well. The province of Valladolid is also where the revered red *Vega Sicilia* is produced. The output of this vineyard is small, so apart from being fairly difficult to find, this wine is expensive.

Each region has its special wines and now with more control and proper labelling, they are improving all the time. Other favourites of mine are the delicious whites from Ribeiro in Galicia which are slightly *pétillant*, and the *Albariños*: watch out, as the latter are slightly acid, and also make you feel rather sleepy. (Asturias, close to Galicia, produces no wine, but does make the best cider in Spain.)

Down in the south the unique wines called sherry need no introduction. Many people, however, don't realize that there is quite such an enormous range, from *fino, amontillado, oloroso,* and *palo cortado* to the cream dessert sherries, plus wines like *Manzanilla* from Sanlúcar and *Montilla* from near Cordoba, which taste similar to sherry. *Malaga* wine, popular in Victorian times, is rather like Madeira. Andalusia is also producing some nice fruity whites.

Spain manufactures almost every drink you can think of, and this includes a vast number of liqueurs (in every monastery you can be sure the monks produce something!). My favourites are the *orujos* from the north of Spain which, being sort of *eau-de-vies*, are not at all sweet. Funnily enough, although in Menorca where, thanks to the English, they make a very good gin, they also have the most delicious herb *aguardiente* liqueurs. Brandies abound throughout the country as a whole. Some are pretty rough, and in most cases they'll probably go into a coffee, the resulting drink known as a *carajillo* (which can also be made with the very popular anise liqueurs). Many of the sherry-makers produce good brandies, as does Torres, up near Barcelona.

FINALMENTE

It only remains to be said that I hope this book will be of help to all those interested in Spain. I hope too that you'll get as much enjoyment out of the food as I did, and wish to for some time to come. 'God willing', as they would say here.

TAPAS · SNACKS

It was a long time before I actually wondered why *tapas* – which literally means 'covers' – were called by that name. I just ate them. In my early days in Spain, a *chato* or tiny glass of wine was always accompanied by a piece of spicy *chorizo* sausage or maybe a fried anchovy. However, we who loved good food used to have our *tapa* routes, which always included *tascas* or bars with some more particular food speciality: maybe snails near the Rastro, the fleamarket; or grilled mushrooms and lamb sweetbreads sautéed in garlic just off the Calle de la Victoria (where one bought the tickets for the bullfights). Quite frequently we'd end up having something slightly more substantial such as white beans and hare in a grotty little place called *El Anarchista* (which unfortunately has disappeared); or go far from where we lived to the Puerta de Toledo and eat the wonderful hake that had been bought from the lorries on their way to the fish market nearby. It may sound a life of gluttony, but it was pretty healthy as we walked for kilometres, and I got to know Madrid pretty well.

Nowadays there are still lots of *tascas* and *mesónes* (olde-worlde bars) in the centre of Madrid which serve *tapas*; there are also more sophisticated establishments around the Calle Serrano which offer more refined types, ranging from minute *vol-au-vents* to *canapés* of smoked fish and caviar. *Tapas* are served all over Spain, but of all the places I've been to, San Sebastian, that beautiful northern city with some of the best restaurants in Spain, gets the prize. Forget about 'lunch', just take a walk around the old quarter, and you'll see what I mean. Try some of the local white *txakolí* wine, or a cider.

However, it is from the other end of Spain that the name *tapa* originated. According to my friends in Seville, there was a smart club there called the *Círculo de Labradores*. In the first decades of this century, women were not allowed in it, and it didn't have a bar. So the lackey was ordered to go to the bar across the street and bring back a tall glass of sherry with a *tapa* over the glass, which would be ham or cheese. The *Círculo* still exists (it now has a bar), as do *tapas*, thank goodness!

FRESHLY PREPARED DISHES AT A BUSY *TAPAS* BAR. (PHOTO BY BRIAN SEED, ASPECT PICTURE LIBRARY)

TORTILLA DE PATATA
Potato Omelette
Nationwide

This is the all-purpose Spanish omelette made from potatoes, a little onion if you like, and eggs. In case you've never seen one, they are round, flat and solid and should be golden brown on top. They can be eaten cold or hot at breakfast, lunch, tea or supper, as a *tapa* or on a picnic. Children love them and if you happen to be going out and have to leave a snack, well, a Spanish omelette is the answer served with a salad. The recipe I am going to give you can be made with three eggs only, but I prefer a nice, moist omelette.

Serves 6–8 as a tapa
1 kg (2¼ lb) potatoes, peeled
1 small onion, peeled (optional)
250 ml (8 fl. oz) olive oil
salt
5 eggs, beaten

Wash and dry the potatoes, then cut in thin slices. If you are using onion, dice it finely.

Heat the oil in a frying pan, add the potatoes and onion, season and cover. Fry gently, moving the pan so that they don't stick. Once the potatoes are cooked – take care they don't become crisp – break them up a bit and then remove from the pan with a slotted spoon and put in the bowl in which you have beaten the eggs. Stir the potatoes around until they are well covered with egg. Add salt to taste.

Remove most of the oil from the frying pan, leaving about 15 ml (1 tbsp) which you heat. Have ready a plate with a slightly larger diameter than the pan. Return the egg and potato mixture to the pan and cook for a few minutes until one side is golden. Next, and this is slightly tricky, slip the omelette out on to your plate, cooked side down, and then slip it back into the pan, cooked side up. Cook until firm.

Your omelette should be about 4 cm (1½ in) thick. If you are serving it for *tapas*, then cut it into squares.

TORTILLA DE PATATA/POTATO OMELETTE

CHAMPIÑÓNES AL AJILLO
Mushrooms with Garlic
Nationwide

This is one of the most popular *tapas*, and it is found in many bars.

Serves 6–8
> 1 kg (2¼ lb) button mushrooms (you can
> use larger ones, chopped)
> juice of ½ lemon
> 150 ml (5 fl. oz) olive oil
> 3 cloves of garlic, peeled and finely chopped
> salt and pepper
> 30 ml (2 tbsp) chopped parsley

Wash the mushrooms well. If they are very dirty put in a bowl of cold water with lemon juice, swill around, then remove and dry in a clean towel.

Heat the oil in either a flameproof earthenware dish or a frying pan and sauté the garlic for a minute or two, then add the mushrooms. Season and cook for about 10 minutes over a medium flame. Increase the heat towards the end. Shake the pan occasionally so that the mushrooms cook evenly.

When they are done sprinkle with chopped parsley and serve.

CHAMPIÑÓNES AL AJILLO/MUSHROOMS WITH GARLIC

CHAMPIÑÓNES AL ESTILO SEGOVIA
Mushrooms with Bacon
Segovia

Another very tasty dish, especially if you can make it with open or flat mushrooms.

Serves 4

> 150 g (5 oz) bacon, rinded and diced
> olive oil (optional)
> 1 clove of garlic, peeled and minced
> 15 ml (1 tbsp) chopped parsley
> 750 g (a good 1½ lb) mushrooms, halved or
> quartered
> 100 ml (3½ fl. oz) dry white wine or dry
> sherry
> salt and pepper

Sauté the bacon in an earthenware casserole or in a frying pan. (Add a little oil if necessary.) When the bacon begins to brown, add the garlic and parsley. Stir in the mushrooms and sauté for about 5 minutes.

Add the wine, salt and freshly ground black pepper and cook until the mushrooms are nearly done, about 5–10 minutes. Increase the heat until the liquid evaporates. Serve immediately.

BERENJENAS FRITAS
Fried Aubergines
Andalusia

This was one of the vegetables brought to Spain by the Arabs. The Andalusians, expert at frying, enthusiastically adopted it, although it took a long time to reach other regions further north.

Serves 4

> 500 g (18 oz) aubergines (the stripey sort
> have fewer seeds)
> salt
> olive or other oil for frying
> plain flour

Peel the aubergines and cut into thin slices. Sprinkle with salt and leave for about an hour to eliminate the water. Dry well.

Heat the oil nice and hot. Dip the aubergines in flour and fry quickly. Drain on kitchen paper. Sprinkle with a little salt and serve immediately.

BERENJENAS FRITAS/FRIED AUBERGINES

ENSALADA DE PIMIENTOS MORRÓNES
Red Pepper Salad
Nationwide

Fresh red peppers prepared this way are an essential part of Spanish cooking, as are the tinned variety. However, there is nothing better than eating them as a salad or a *tapa*, using the dressing you prefer.

Roast the peppers well until charred black on all sides. Do this in a very hot oven, on a hotplate, or under the grill, turning them occasionally. If they are large, this could take about 20 minutes. Put them into a covered pot for a few minutes until they are cool enough to handle (or until you want to prepare them).

Peel them, cut them in half, remove the cores and seeds, and cut the flesh into long strips. Arrange on a dish and dress simply with oil, vinegar, salt and pepper, and perhaps a little chopped garlic.

A RIVER LANDSCAPE IN THE NAVARRA REGION, NOTED FOR ITS VINEYARDS AND ASPARAGUS CULTIVATION.

PIPIRRANA
Vegetable Salad
Andalusia

An extremely simple, refreshing salad eaten in Andalusia usually as a *tapa* or with fried fish. *Pipirrana* is the name used in Malaga and Jaen; the name and the ingredients vary slightly from place to place.

Serves 4

1 cucumber, peeled and diced
1 green pepper, seeded and diced
1 onion, peeled and diced
3 medium tomatoes, diced

DRESSING
salt and pepper
30 ml (2 tbsp) wine vinegar
90 ml (6 tbsp) olive oil

If you want to make a larger amount, simply double the ingredients.

Mix the vegetables together and put in a glass bowl.

Make the dressing by dissolving the salt and pepper in the vinegar, then stir in the oil slowly. Pour over the salad and leave for at least half an hour before serving nice and cold.

ENSALADA DE PIMIENTOS MORRÓNES/RED PEPPER SALAD

GAMBAS AL AJILLO
Shrimps with Garlic
Nationwide

When you are using fresh shrimps remember that 500 g (18 oz) will reduce to about 250 g (9 oz) after you have peeled them.

Serves 4

> 60–75 ml (4–5 tbsp) olive oil
> 6 cloves of garlic, peeled and sliced
> 250 g (9 oz) peeled shrimps
> 1 dried red chilli pepper, cut in 3 pieces,
> seeds removed
> salt

Heat the oil, preferably in a round flameproof earthenware dish, and fry the garlic. Add the shrimps, chilli and some salt, and stir with a wooden spoon. Cover, cook for about 4–5 minutes, and serve sizzling from the same dish.

MEJILLONES A LA VINAGRETA/MUSSELS IN
VINAIGRETTE

MEJILLONES A LA VINAGRETA
Mussels in Vinaigrette
Nationwide

You're likely to find this in almost any coastal bar or restaurant. Mussels are now farmed in many places, on *mejilloneras* or floating platforms.

Serves 6–8

> 2 kg (4 lb, 7 oz) mussels
> salt and pepper
>
> VINAIGRETTE SAUCE
> 90 ml (6 tbsp) olive oil
> 45 ml (3 tbsp) wine vinegar
> 15 ml (1 tbsp) finely chopped onion
> 15 ml (1 tbsp) finely chopped tinned or
> home-prepared sweet red peppers
> (see page 22)
> 15 ml (1 tbsp) finely chopped parsley

Scrub and scrape the mussels well and remove the beards. Throw away any mussels that are open and do not close when tapped with a knife. Wash well in water and drain.

Place the mussels in a saucepan with 250 ml (8 fl. oz) of cold water and a pinch of salt. Put over high heat, cover and bring to the boil. Remove the mussels as they open and leave to cool. Throw away any that do not open.

Make the vinaigrette sauce by mixing the oil, vinegar, onion, sweet red peppers, parsley, and some salt and pepper in a bowl. Arrange the mussels in a dish and spoon the sauce over each one.

MEJILLONES FRITOS
Mussels Fried in Breadcrumbs
Madrid

If you happen to be in Madrid, do go to *La Trucha* ('trout') and try the Béchamel mussels below!

Serves 6

1.5 kg (3 lb, 5 oz) mussels
2 eggs
salt and pepper
oil for deep-frying
fine dry breadcrumbs for coating

Clean and cook the mussels as in the preceding recipe. Once they are cooked remove them from their shells and dry well, either in a cloth or kitchen paper.

Beat the eggs, and add a pinch of salt and pepper. Heat the oil until nice and hot then dip each mussel in the egg and then breadcrumbs. Fry until golden. Serve immediately with any sauce you fancy such as spicy tomato or maybe a garlic mayonnaise, or simply with a squeeze of lemon juice.

Slightly more time-consuming are mussels which you chop with hard-boiled egg, mix into a Béchamel sauce, spoon back into the shells, sprinkle with breadcrumbs and put under a hot grill for a few minutes. Well worth the effort, though!

GAMBAS A LA PLANCHA
Grilled Prawns
Nationwide

The larger prawns are the best for grilling. In Spain *'a la plancha'* literally means cooking 'on the plate', or cooking on an oiled pan or griddle. Look for this dish at the coast or in major cities, as it might not always feature in smaller places in central Spain.

Serves 4

500 g (18 oz) uncooked prawns
1 clove of garlic, peeled
45 ml (3 tbsp) olive oil
juice of 1 lemon
salt and pepper

Do *not* peel the prawns.

Crush the garlic and stir it into a mixture of the oil and lemon juice. Season with salt and pepper. Brush the prawns with this mixture and place them on a hot griddle or frying pan. As soon as they begin to cook turn them over and sprinkle with more oil and lemon mixture. They will soon turn a bright pinkish red. Depending on their size they'll take about 10 minutes in all to cook.

The best way to eat them is with your fingers, peeling off the shells and savouring each prawn to the full.

ALMEJAS A LA MARINERA
Clams with White Wine and Garlic
Coastal Areas

This dish can be found in the simplest bar or the grandest restaurant, as a *tapa* or a first course.

Serves 4

> 750 g (a good 1½ lb) medium to small clams
> salt and pepper
> 45 ml (3 tbsp) olive oil
> 1 small onion, peeled and finely chopped
> 3 cloves of garlic, peeled and minced
> 15 ml (1 tbsp) plain flour
> 100 ml (3½ fl. oz) dry white wine
> a pinch of paprika
> 1 bay leaf

Wash the clams well. Leave them in cold water to which you have added a little salt for about an hour to get rid of any grit they may have in them.

Heat the oil in a frying pan. Add the onion and garlic and sauté until golden brown. Add the clams and cook over a medium heat until the shells open. Add the flour and stir in well. Pour in the wine, add the paprika, bay leaf and some salt and pepper. Continue cooking for a further 5 minutes.

Remove the bay leaf and serve the clams in the sauce. Half the fun is to eat the clam and then spoon up some sauce using the shell as a spoon.

BOQUERÓNES FRITOS
Fried Fresh Anchovies
Andalusia

Fresh anchovies may be difficult to find, but if you do come across them, this simple recipe is delicious. In Andalusia, they pick up and fry five at a time!

> fresh anchovies
> salt
> plain flour
> olive oil

The smallest fish are the best for frying. Remove the insides and wash and dry well. Sprinkle with salt and dip in flour.

Fry quickly in plenty of hot oil, drain well and serve immediately.

THE ROMANESQUE CHURCH OF SAN PABLO IN PEÑAFIEL, OLD CASTILE.

BOQUERÓNES EN VINAGRE
Fresh Anchovies Marinated in Vinegar
Nationwide

Marinating fish has always been a good way of preserving it – as well as a good way of eating it!

Serves 6–8

> *500 g (18 oz) fresh anchovies*
> *2 cloves of garlic, peeled and sliced*
> *½ onion, peeled and sliced*
> *4 bay leaves*
> *salt*
> *250 ml (8 fl. oz) wine vinegar*
> *30 ml (2 tbsp) olive oil*
> *30 ml (2 tbsp) chopped parsley*

Wash and scale the anchovies. Remove the heads, cut the bodies along the stomach, and remove the backbones by taking hold of the tail and pulling it. Clean very well, washing several times, and cut off the tails. Dry well and place the fillets, skin side down, in a shallow dish.

Put the garlic, onion, bay leaves and some salt into the vinegar and pour this mixture over the fish so that it is well covered. Leave for at least 5 hours or overnight.

Before serving, cover the dish with a plate and pour off the vinegar. Discard the onion, bay and garlic. Pour the olive oil over the fish. Sprinkle with parsley and more chopped garlic if you wish, and they are ready to eat.

THE *MÉSON LA FRAGNA* IN VALLADOLID IS ONE OF THE BEST RESTAURANTS IN OLD CASTILE, RETAINING ITS TRADITIONAL *ASADOR* OR ROASTING OVEN TO COOK REGIONAL FOODS.

BOQUERÓNES EN VINAGRE/FRESH ANCHOVIES MARINATED IN VINEGAR

(*OVERLEAF*) THE VILLAGE OF CASARAS, TYPICAL OF SOUTHERN ANDALUSIA, WHERE SUCH *TAPAS* RECIPES AS FRIED AUBERGINES, VEGETABLE SALAD AND FRIED FRESH ANCHOVIES ORIGINATE. (PHOTO BY BOB DAVIS, ASPECT PICTURE LIBRARY)

SALPICON DE MARISCOS
Shellfish Salad
Nationwide

It causes me a certain amount of amusement to include this recipe because one of the doyennes of Spanish cookery books at the beginning of this century, the Countess of Pardo Bazán, described the *salpicon* as 'one of the most usual but least recommendable of Spanish dressings'. However don't be put off, as she was really referring to the fact that, as it is a piquant sauce, it should be used with more insipid tasting foods and not, for example, with delicately flavoured lobster. Pieces of octopus or squid are good in a *salpicon*, as are pieces of angler (monk) fish – almost anything or everything can be used.

Serves 4

> 200 g (7 oz) cooked shrimps or prawns, peeled
> 250 g (9 oz) shelled mussels, cooked
>
> DRESSING
> salt and pepper
> 30 ml (2 tbsp) wine vinegar
> 90 ml (6 tbsp) olive oil
> 1 onion, peeled and finely chopped
> 30 ml (2 tbsp) finely chopped parsley
> 2 hard-boiled eggs, finely chopped

Put the shrimps and mussels into a dish.

Make your dressing in a bowl by first dissolving salt and pepper to taste in the vinegar and then adding the oil slowly, stirring all the time. Add the onion, parsley and egg and pour over the shrimps and mussels. Mix well and serve.

FRESH SPANISH BREADS TO MOP UP THE *TAPAS* SAUCES

SALPICON DE MARISCOS/SHELLFISH SALAD

·ENTRADAS·
FIRST COURSES

THE CENTRAL SQUARE OF THE OLD ROMAN TOWN OF
CALAHORRA IN RIOJA, WHERE THE DELICIOUS
MENESTRA DE VERDURAS IS PREPARED IN THE HEART
OF THE WINE-GROWING REGION.

Small portions of these first courses can also be eaten as *tapas*, and of course larger helpings of *tapas* can be eaten as first courses.

As a lot of the recipes throughout the book include peppers, I'd like to explain that *pimientos* in Spanish refers to the large and small red and green varieties which can be hot or sweet. Some sorts of green peppers turn red when they mature. The fatter smaller ones are called bell peppers, and can be used in place of the longer pointed ones; the latter are best for frying whilst the former are good stuffed. The big red peppers are nearly always grilled or roasted so that they char and their skins are easily removed. These are the peppers that are tinned and known as *pimientos morrónes*. Also of frequent use in Spain are *ñoras* or *pimientos choriceros* which are dried sweet peppers, and of course the hot chilli, small *guindilla*.

For frying things such as croquettes you can use any sort of oil, but if you want to keep the Spanish flavour, I would always use olive oil if it remains in the dish. *Habas con jamon*, for example, would not be the same without it.

HIDDEN IN THE MOUNTAINS OF CATALONIA ARE THE
RUINS OF THE OLD ABBEY OF SCALA DEI, BACKED BY
THE SIERRA DE MONTSANT.

PATATAS GUISADAS CON CHIRLAS
Potatoes with Clams
Nationwide

This common dish is fairly substantial, a cross between a soup and a stew.

Serves 4

> *250 g (9 oz) small clams*
> *salt*
> *50 ml (2 fl. oz) white wine*
> *50 ml (2 fl. oz) olive oil*
> *1 medium onion, peeled and diced*
> *2 medium tomatoes, skinned, seeded and chopped*
> *1 kg (2¼ lb) potatoes, peeled and cut into chunks*
> *1.25 litres (2¼ pints) water*
> *1 clove of garlic, peeled and roughly chopped*
> *5 ml (1 tsp) roughly chopped parsley*
> *4 or 5 strands of saffron*

Wash the clams well in cold water with some salt. Change the water a couple of times. Put them in a saucepan and barely cover with cold water. Add the wine and a teaspoon of salt. Bring to the boil and as soon as the clams open remove from the heat. Strain off the liquid and keep. Remove the clams from their shells and keep in the liquid.

Heat the oil in a frying pan and sauté the onion until it is transparent, then add the tomatoes and continue to sauté for another 5 minutes. Next put the contents of the frying pan into a large saucepan, add the potatoes, cover with the measured water and bring to the boil.

Meanwhile crush the garlic with a little salt, the parsley and saffron. Add a tablespoonful of the liquid from the clams, mix well and stir into the potatoes with the rest of the clam liquid (keep the clams to one side). Cover and simmer until the potatoes are done, about half an hour. Heat the clams through in the soup just before serving.

You can thicken the liquid by puréeing a potato or two and adding them to the saucepan. If on the other hand you find you have *too little* liquid you can always add more hot water when the potatoes are cooking.

VEGETABLES AND PULSES FREQUENTLY USED FOR FIRST-COURSE DISHES

PATATAS CON COSTILLAS
Potatoes with Spare Ribs
Nationwide

Potatoes are served as a first course in Spain done in innumerable ways, and in fact a dish like this one is actually more than sufficient for lunch. A chilli pepper makes it nice and spicy if you like things hot.

Please note that if you use *fresh* meat, then when you add the water add more herbs such as thyme and oregano.

Serves 4

30 ml (2 tbsp) oil
300 g (11 oz) marinated or fresh spare ribs,
cut into pieces
2 cloves of garlic, peeled and chopped
1 medium onion, peeled and diced
1 green pepper, seeded and chopped
250 g (9 oz) tomatoes, roughly chopped
1 litre (1¾ pints) meat stock or water
salt and pepper
1 bay leaf
1 kg (2¼ lb) potatoes, peeled and cut into
thick chunks
5 ml (1 tsp) chopped parsley

Heat the oil in a casserole, add the spare ribs and sauté them for a few minutes. Add the garlic, stir in well and then add the onion. Sauté together gently for about 10 minutes until the onion is transparent but not golden. Add the pepper and tomatoes and cook for another 5 minutes. Pour over the hot stock or water, season to taste, and add the bay leaf.

Bring to the boil, cover, lower the heat and simmer until the meat is nearly cooked – about 20–30 minutes. Add the potatoes and cook until done, another 15–20 minutes. Test the seasoning and thickness of the liquid. If you want to thicken it more, purée one or two of the potatoes and return to the casserole. Sprinkle with parsley and serve.

JUST TO THE NORTH OF TARRAGONA, IN CATALONIA, LIES THE ROMAN AQUEDUCT, PUENTE DEL DIABLO (DEVIL'S BRIDGE).

ONE OF THE CAFÉS IN THE PLAZA MAYOR IN MADRID, WHERE CONVERSATION MIGHT WELL BE ACCOMPANIED BY PLATES OF SCRAMBLED EGGS WITH ASPARAGUS.

LENTEJAS GUISADAS
Stewed Lentils
Nationwide

Lentils are eaten all over Spain in different ways, and I have to confess to a passion for them. There is nothing better on a cold winter's day. Depending on what ingredients you use, they are more or less digestible. Obviously if you make them with lots of *chorizo* sausage and pork, they are a meal in themselves, but if you just use vegetables then they make an excellent first course. I always make large quantities so there is plenty left over as they not only reheat well, but make an excellent purée. I prefer the larger, greeny-brown variety of lentils most commonly used in Spain. Also I find it's best to make them the day before as they improve in flavour and take on a better consistency.

Serves 6

600 g (1 lb, 5 oz) lentils
about 2 litres (3½ pints) water
1 medium onion, peeled and halved
2 cloves of garlic, peeled
1 bay leaf
2 sprigs of parsley
a ham bone, piece of gammon and spare ribs (optional)
4 carrots, scraped
4 potatoes, peeled and quartered
30 ml (2 tbsp) olive oil
1 medium tomato, skinned, seeded and chopped
5 ml (1 tsp) paprika
salt and pepper

Put the lentils to soak in cold water for about 2 hours or leave them overnight. Be sure to remove any little stones and any lentils that rise to the surface. Drain them.

Put the lentils in a saucepan and cover with the measured cold water. Add half the onion, a clove of garlic, the bay leaf and a sprig of parsley (and the optional meat if you are using it). Bring to the boil, cover, and cook slowly for about an hour. Add the carrots and potatoes and allow to finish cooking, about another 20–30 minutes.

Meanwhile, in a frying pan heat the oil and fry the other half of the onion, which you've chopped, plus the tomato. After about 10 minutes remove from the heat, and stir in the paprika. Stir well and mix into the lentils when the potatoes have cooked.

Crush the remaining garlic and parsley and some salt in a little of the soup in a pestle and mortar. Return to the saucepan, cook for another 10 minutes and serve in a tureen after removing the ham bone, onion half, bay leaf and whole clove of garlic. Chop the carrot and potato into small chunks.

In Spain people love to add a dash of vinegar to their helpings.

LENTEJAS GUISADAS/STEWED LENTILS AND *FABES ESTOFADAS*/STEWED WHITE BEANS (SEE PAGE 56)

MENESTRA DE VERDURAS
Mixed Vegetables
La Rioja

Menestra de verduras, which means literally a combination of vegetables, is eaten in most parts of Spain and, like many other things, varies considerably from place to place. I think the best *menestra* I have ever eaten was at *Casa Terete* in Haro in the heart of the wine-growing region of La Rioja Alta. Funnily enough I have never eaten any similar dish abroad, the reason being perhaps that in Spain vegetables are nearly always eaten as a separate dish, whilst in other countries they are used more as an accompaniment for main courses. If you want to order this dish in Spain, always ask first if the vegetables are fresh and not tinned or frozen. Beware, vegetarians, if you are thinking this is the perfect dish for you as tiny diced pieces of ham are often added to it.

The quantities in the recipe are entirely optional, use more or less of the vegetables you prefer.

Serves 4

4 carrots, scraped and halved
250 g (9 oz) green beans, stringed and cut into 2.5 cm (1 in) pieces
½ small cauliflower, broken into florets
2 leeks, cleaned and cut into pieces
150 g (5 oz) shelled peas
150 g (5 oz) shelled broad beans
4 artichoke hearts, halved or quartered, depending on size
salt and pepper
olive oil
65 g (2½ oz) cured ham, diced
1 small onion, peeled and finely chopped
1 clove of garlic, peeled and minced (optional)
1 egg, beaten
flour for dusting
oil for frying

Bring about 2.5 cm (1 in) of water to boil in a large, fairly shallow saucepan. Add all the vegetables (except for the onion and garlic), plus some seasoning. Cover and simmer, being careful not to overcook. Remove the vegetables as they are done, drain and keep warm.

Take a flameproof earthenware pen or casserole and heat 45 ml (3 tbsp) of olive oil in it. Add the ham and sauté for a minute, then add the onion and garlic if you are using it. Cook until the onion is transparent. Stir in all the vegetables, except for the artichokes (which you dip in the flour and beaten egg and fry separately in hot olive oil). Sauté the vegetables for 3–4 minutes, then arrange nicely in a dish with the artichokes and serve.

The cauliflower could also be fried in batter. Spinach is sometimes used rolled up into little cakes and dipped in flour and egg and fried. Red peppers, asparagus, a garnish of hard-boiled egg, it is hard to say which way is best . . .

MENESTRA DE VERDURAS/MIXED VEGETABLES

(*OVERLEAF*) SHEEP GRAZE PEACEFULLY ACROSS THE ROUGH GRASSLANDS OF CATALONIA.

PISTO MANCHEGO
Spanish Vegetable Stew
La Mancha

This extremely versatile vegetable dish is typical of La Mancha, the region made famous by Cervantes' novel about Don Quixote. It is similar to the French *ratatouille*, and is eaten all over Spain (although it has different names in different parts). It is usually eaten as a first course, but as it is pretty filling, it's perfect for a light lunch or supper. Try it with a couple of fried eggs or with eggs scrambled into it.

It is worth making large quantities of *pisto* as it keeps well, reheats wonderfully and can be varied – for example, add a little cooked rice to it, perfect for vegetarians, or a small tin of tunny fish.

Serves 6
> *1.5 kg (3½ lb) courgettes*
> *2 large onions, peeled and diced*
> *1 clove of garlic, peeled and diced*
> *500 g (18 oz) green peppers, seeded and chopped*
> *1 kg (2¼ lb) tomatoes, skinned, seeded and chopped*
> *90 ml (6 tbsp) olive oil*
> *salt, pepper and sugar*

Prepare the vegetables first. In Spain the courgettes are peeled, but if they are the small variety I leave the skins on as they are tastier. Dice them fairly large.

Heat the oil gently in a large casserole. Cook the onion, garlic and peppers until the onion is transparent. Add the tomatoes and cook for another 5 minutes, stirring all the time with a wooden spoon. Add the courgettes and stir in well. Season with salt and pepper and I usually add a pinch of sugar as well.

Cook over a low flame with the lid on for about 20 minutes, stirring occasionally, until the *pisto* is cooked, not overcooked! If it is too liquid, remove the lid, turn up the heat and cook for a few minutes so that the surplus juice evaporates.

ACROSS THE RIVER FROM THE TOWN OF ESTELLA IN NAVARRA, IN THE HAMLET OF AYEGUI, IS THE MONASTERIO DE IRACHE, WHICH BECAME A BENEDICTINE UNIVERSITY IN THE SIXTEENTH CENTURY.

PISTO MANCHEGO/SPANISH VEGETABLE STEW

ESPINACAS A LA CATALANA
Catalan Spinach
Barcelona

This is one of the most popular Catalan vegetable starters.

Serves 4

> *45 ml (3 tbsp) Malaga raisins or sultanas*
> *2 kg (a scant 4½ lb) fresh spinach, washed*
> *and trimmed, tough stalks removed*
> *salt and pepper*
> *100 ml (3½ fl oz) olive oil*
> *1 clove of garlic, peeled and chopped*
> *45 ml (3 tbsp) pine kernels*

Soak the raisins in warm water, whilst preparing and cooking the spinach. Boil it in as little salted water as possible for about 5 minutes. Drain well and press the spinach between two plates to get rid of surplus water, then chop it slightly. Remove stalks from raisins and cut in half.

Heat the oil in a frying pan and when it is hot add the chopped garlic. After about a minute, add the spinach, pine kernels and raisins. Season with salt and pepper and sauté for about 5 minutes. Serve immediately.

COLIFLOR SALTEADO
Cauliflower Sautéed in Garlic
Nationwide

Sautéing with garlic is a common way of eating vegetables in Spain, and it is particularly suited to cauliflower and Brussels sprouts. In Spain people tend to cook their vegetables much longer than I do.

Serves 4

> *1 medium cauliflower*
> *2 cloves of garlic, peeled and sliced*
> *100 ml (3½ fl. oz) olive oil*
> *salt and white pepper*
> *5 ml (1 tsp) chopped parsley*

Boil the cauliflower in lightly salted water, being careful not to overcook it. Drain off the water and break into florets.

Heat the garlic in the oil. Dry the cauliflower in a clean towel and sauté in the oil and garlic until golden. Season with salt and pepper and sprinkle with parsley.

ESPINACAS A LA CATALANA/CATALAN SPINACH

COLIFLOR EN SALSA VINAGRETA
Cauliflower in Vinaigrette Sauce
Nationwide

Another delicious way of eating cauliflower, especially if you want to prepare an easy first course.

Serves 4

1 medium cauliflower
salt
½ small onion, peeled and chopped
2–3 gherkins, finely chopped
1 clove of garlic, peeled and finely chopped
pepper
30 ml (2 tbsp) wine vinegar
90 ml (6 tbsp) olive oil

Boil the cauliflower in boiling salted water until barely tender. Drain and leave to cool.

Make the sauce by mixing all the remaining ingredients in the vinegar and then adding the oil.

Serve the cauliflower broken into florets on a napkin in a dish, with the sauce handed separately.

Depending on the vinegar you use and the strength you like it, you can use more or less, and obviously make more by increasing the quantities.

ALCACHOFAS ESTOFADAS
Artichokes Braised in White Wine
Andalusia

What they would probably use in Andalusia is some of the local Montilla wine, which is similar to sherry.

Serves 4

6 artichokes
50 ml (2 fl. oz) olive oil
1 small onion, peeled and finely chopped
2 cloves of garlic, peeled and finely sliced
200 ml (7 fl. oz) white wine or dry sherry
salt
freshly grated nutmeg

Remove the stalks and outer leaves from the artichokes and wash well. Cut each one into four pieces. Heat the oil in a casserole and gently sauté the onion and garlic for about 4 minutes. Add the artichokes and wine and season with salt and nutmeg. Cook gently until done, from 20–40 minutes, depending on size and type. (Test by pulling a leaf; if done it will come away easily.) If the liquid should reduce too much you can add a little water.

ALCACHOFAS REBOZADAS
Artichokes in Batter
Nationwide

Frying in batter is a very popular way of eating vegetables in Spain. Cauliflower is also good.

Serves 4

8 fairly small artichokes
juice of 1 lemon
salt and pepper
seasoned plain flour for coating
2 eggs, beaten
1 litre (1¾ pints) vegetable or olive oil for
frying

Cut the stalks off the artichokes and peel off the
tough outside leaves. Cut in half lengthwise and put
in cold water to which you have added some of the
lemon juice. Bring plenty of water to the boil in a
saucepan, add salt, a little lemon juice (or a teaspoon of vinegar, these acids prevent the artichokes
going black), and the artichokes. Cover and lower
the heat and cook for about half an hour or until they
are done, which is when you can pull out a leaf
easily. Drain well and, if necessary, dry in a towel as
they tend to retain water.

Dip the artichokes in the seasoned flour and
then in the beaten egg. Heat the oil until it is hot –
you can test it with a bit of bread which should
become golden immediately if the temperature is
correct – then fry the artichokes until golden. Drain
on absorbent paper and serve immediately.

HABAS CON JAMÓN
Broad Beans with Ham
Nationwide

You will notice no water is used in cooking the
beans. This is due to the fact that in many parts of
Spain there was and is a shortage of water. As a result
vegetables were seldom boiled and other means of
cooking them were devised.

Serves 4

100 ml (3½ fl. oz) olive oil
1 kg (2¼ lb) young broad beans, shelled
100 g (4 oz) cured ham, diced
salt

Heat the oil in a casserole. Add the beans and sauté
for about 5 minutes, stirring constantly. Add the
ham and continue cooking until the beans are done,
about another 5 minutes (depending on the beans).
Season if necessary (the ham may be fairly salty),
and serve.

ESCALIVADA
Mixed Vegetable Salad
Catalonia

I'd been in Spain for a number of years before I discovered *escalivada* at the *masia* (country house) of some Catalan friends. Without a doubt it is one of my favourite summer dishes, and fortunately now appears more on menus in other parts of the country. It is a sort of salad made from aubergines, red peppers, tomatoes and onions. The secret lies in charring them before they are peeled which gives a very special flavour.

At smarter restaurants in Catalonia which go in for *nouvelle cuisine*, I have recently eaten a delicious mousse made from *escalivada*.

Serves 4–6

> *4 medium aubergines*
> *4 medium red peppers*
> *olive oil*
> *4 medium onions*
> *4 medium tomatoes*
> *chopped garlic (optional)*
> *salt and pepper*
> *vinegar or lemon juice*

Rub the outside of the aubergines and peppers with olive oil and place under a hot grill (you probably don't have a charcoal or wood fire available!). Turn them frequently until they are charred black on all sides. Remove and place in a covered dish. Do the same with the onions, and lastly the tomatoes which will take far less time. You will also have equally good results using a hot oven (200°C/400°F/Gas 6). Leave the vegetables to cool for at least half an hour or more in a covered pot.

Peel off the skins, and remove seeds from peppers. (Sometimes I peel the onions before charring them and also use a slightly lower heat as they take slightly longer to cook.) Cut the aubergines and peppers into strips. Slice the onion and tomatoes roughly and arrange nicely on a serving dish placing all the onion together, the tomatoes, aubergines and so on. Sprinkle with chopped garlic, salt, pepper and olive oil. Add a little vinegar or lemon if you prefer.

I have also eaten *escalivada* with cold boiled potatoes which are added at the last minute with the dressing.

ESCALIVADA/MIXED VEGETABLE SALAD AND
CROQUETAS DE JAMON/HAM CROQUETTES (SEE PAGE
59)

FABES ESTOFADAS
Stewed White Beans
Asturias

This is a cross between a soup and a stew, but it makes a good first course or perfectly substantial main course as the beans are full of protein. Follow it with a piece of cheese and your meal will be complete. If you can find the Asturian *fabes*, use them, otherwise lima or butter beans will do. I like to make my *fabes* the day before, as not only does the flavour improve but so does the consistency. However, if you want to thicken the soup you can either dissolve a little flour in some of the liquid and then return it to the pot and cook for about 10 minutes longer or, alternatively, purée a few of the beans and return them to the saucepan.

Serves 4

> 500 g (18 oz) dried white beans
> 1.5 litres (2½ pints) water
> 50 ml (2 fl. oz) olive oil
> 1 onion, peeled and roughly sliced
> 1 clove of garlic, peeled
> ½ tinned red pepper, chopped
> 1 medium tomato
> 5 ml (1 tsp) paprika
> salt
> a sprig of parsley

Soak the beans overnight in plenty of cold water. When you are going to cook them, drain and re-cover with water; bring to the boil and then throw away this water (the reason being that it makes them more digestible).

Cover the beans with the measured water, and add all the remaining ingredients. Bring to the boil, turn down the heat and simmer until done. The time depends very much on the type of beans you are using, but it should take about an hour. Add more water if necessary, the beans should have a fair amount of liquid.

BERENJENAS CON ANCHOAS
Aubergines with Anchovies
Catalonia

This simple and delicious recipe was given to me by Jaume Subirós, the owner of the Hotel Ampurdán in Gerona. The Empordá area is renowned for its cuisine and one of the culinary pioneers of our age was the father-in-law of Subirós, Josep Mercader. He was an innovator in the sixties when Spanish cooking in general was at a low ebb, with a gift for combining the old and the new, or rather giving new life to old traditions. When Mercader died his son-in-law continued to run the hotel and restaurant, a perfect place to stop at if you are driving down from France. (Don't be put off by the hotel's rather functional appearance!)

The name of this dish in Catalan, *Alberginies farcides amb Anxoves* literally means 'Aubergines stuffed with anchovies'; this is slightly misleading as actually the anchovies go on top and not into the aubergines.

Serves 4

> 4 medium to small aubergines
> salt and pepper
> 50 ml (2 fl. oz) olive oil
> 1 clove of garlic, peeled
> 2 tomatoes, peeled, seeded and chopped

56

THE CLIFFS FALLING AWAY AT THE EDGE OF THE TOWN
OF RONDA IN ANDALUSIA.

a pinch of sugar
a sprig of parsley
25 g (1 oz) fresh breadcrumbs
8 anchovy fillets, cut in half lengthwise

Cut the aubergines in half lengthwise and sprinkle them with salt. Leave for 30 minutes and then wash away any surplus liquid. Using a small spoon, scoop out the insides and put this and the shells to one side.

Heat 30 ml (2 tbsp) of the oil and sauté the garlic until golden. Remove and keep to one side. Next add the tomatoes, the insides of the aubergines, the sugar and some salt and pepper to the pan. Sauté gently, stirring frequently, until you have a thickish sauce. This will take about 30 minutes.

Finely chop or mince the garlic and the parsley and mix with the breadcrumbs.

Spoon the sauce into the aubergine shells, and arrange two pieces of anchovy fillet on each half. Sprinkle the *persillada*, as the breadcrumb mixture is called, over each aubergine half, moisten with a few drops of oil and brown under the preheated grill for about 5 minutes. You can either eat them immediately, or they are very good cold as well.

TORTILLA DE ESPINACAS
Spinach Omelette
Nationwide

There are a number of other delicious omelettes which can be made like the *tortilla de patata* on page 18, but using different ingredients. Spinach omelette is one of my favourites, either eaten on its own or forming part of a sort of cake made from three omelettes, say – spinach, potato and tunny fish – placed on top of each other and served with tomato sauce.

Serves 2

250 g (9 oz) frozen spinach
salt and pepper
4 eggs
a little olive oil

Boil the spinach quickly in very little salted water for 2–3 minutes. Drain it and then – most important – squeeze it between two plates so that all the moisture is eliminated.

Whisk the eggs in a bowl, then stir in the seasoning and spinach. Meanwhile heat about 15 ml (1 tbsp) of olive oil in a frying pan. Pour in your mixture and spread over the pan. This mustn't be too wide as, remember, the omelette is supposed to be about 3–4 cm (1–1½ in) thick. Cook on one side, then slip out on to a plate. Slide back into the pan, cooked side up, and cook until done. It would be very Spanish to sauté your spinach in a little oil and garlic before making the omelette.

HUEVOS A LA FLAMENCA
Flamenco Eggs
Andalusia

This is one of the best-known Spanish dishes abroad. It is a colourful dish of Andalusian origin, although some say it was created in Seville. The ingredients can be varied so if you haven't got asparagus, you could use artichoke hearts or even chopped runner beans.

Serves 4

150 g (5 oz) cured ham, diced
8 thin slices chorizo *sausage*
8 eggs
8 asparagus tips, cooked or tinned
1 sweet red pepper, seeded and cut into
strips
salt and pepper
a pinch of paprika
15 ml (1 tbsp) chopped parsley

TOMATO SAUCE
30 ml (2 tbsp) olive oil
1 medium onion, peeled and finely chopped
500 g (18 oz) tomatoes, skinned, seeded
and chopped
45 ml (3 tbsp) cooked peas

First make the tomato sauce. Heat the oil in a pan and fry the onion until transparent. Add the tomatoes and some salt and pepper. Cover and cook for about 10 minutes.

Meanwhile, in another pan, gently sauté the ham and *chorizo* in a little more oil for a few minutes.

Add the peas to the tomato sauce and pour into individual shallow baking dishes. Break 2 eggs into each dish. Arrange the asparagus tips, *chorizo* mixture and red pepper around the eggs. Sprinkle with salt, pepper, paprika and parsley. Place the dishes in a hot oven, preheated to 200°C (400°F) Gas 6, and cook until the egg whites are set (don't let the yolks get hard), about 7 minutes.

If you want to add garlic to your tomato sauce, feel free. It's a matter of taste.

HUEVOS REVUELTOS CON ESPARRAGOS
Scrambled Eggs and Asparagus
Madrid

An apparently simple dish that can go very wrong if you don't make it properly. Scrambled eggs need constant attention and patience, as there is no speeding up the process if you want to get the consistency right. It is a very popular dish in Spain and more often than not is made with the thin, green asparagus known as *esparragos trigueros* (wild asparagus). If you have a few cold asparagus spears left over it is a delicious way of using them up. In Spain oil is used instead of butter.

Serves 2

65 g (2½ oz) asparagus
45 g (1¾ oz) butter
4 large eggs, beaten
salt and pepper

Cut off the woody ends of the asparagus, scrape if necessary, wash and cook in boiling water for about

8 minutes. If you are using wild asparagus (or sprue) they'll only take about 5 minutes to cook. Drain well and cut into pieces about 2 cm (¾ in) long.

Melt the butter in a thick saucepan or frying pan over a low flame. Season the beaten eggs well, and add to the pan. Stir with a wooden spoon until they begin to thicken. At this point add the asparagus and continue to stir until the eggs are set. I like mine just set and as liquid as possible, so I remove them from the flame just before they are done and continue to stir until the consistency is right. Serve *immediately*.

CROQUETAS DE JAMON
Ham Croquettes
Nationwide

This same recipe can be used with innumerable ingredients such as cold chicken, tunny fish or simply hard-boiled eggs. The secret lies in making a good, creamy Béchamel and then frying the croquettes quickly in hot oil. I always use butter for the Béchamel, although in Spain oil is often used instead. If you are serving croquettes as a first or main course, tomato sauce goes well with them. If you are serving them as a *tapa*, make them half the size, the normal size being that of a small egg.

It is not as easy as it was once to find good *croquetas* in Madrid, as sometimes commercially frozen ones are served. So always ask first at a bar or restaurant if they are home-made. *Principe de Viana* (which has one star in the *Michelin Guide*) offers some of the best *croquetas* I have ever had, made from dried cod and shrimps and served with a tarragon-flavoured Hollandaise sauce.

Makes about 36 croquettes
150 g (5 oz) butter
150 g (5 oz) ham, finely chopped
120 g (4½ oz) plain flour
1 litre (1¾ pints) hot milk
salt and pepper
5 ml (1 tsp) freshly grated nutmeg
plain flour for coating
3 or 4 eggs, beaten
dried breadcrumbs for coating
oil for frying

Gently heat the butter in a thick saucepan, then with a wooden spoon stir in the ham and flour. Continue to stir for about a minute. Next stir in a little of the hot milk. If the mixture thickens too fast remove from the heat and add more milk and stir until it is smooth. (If you are using hard-boiled eggs or tunny fish, add to the sauce when it is cooked.) Gradually add the rest of the milk, some salt and pepper and the nutmeg. (Taste before salting as the ham could contain a lot.) Allow to cook fast for about 10 minutes. By now the mixture should have thickened, so pour it into a tin or baking dish and leave to get cool. This will take about 2 hours.

Divide up into portions, roll each one into a ball, then form into small egg shapes. Dip in flour and beaten egg and then in the breadcrumbs. Fry in hot oil until golden on all sides. Drain on absorbent paper and serve.

MAHONESA
Mayonnaise
Menorca

One of the great sauces of the world, mayonnaise is supposed to have originated in Mahon on the island of Menorca.

When making mayonnaise make sure that the ingredients are at room temperature otherwise it may curdle.

Serves 6

juice of 1 lemon
1 egg yolk
salt and pepper
250 ml (8 fl. oz) olive oil
15 ml (1 tbsp) hot water

Put the lemon juice and egg yolk in a glass bowl and beat well with a wooden spoon. Beat in a little salt and pepper then, drop by drop, beat in the olive oil. If the mayonnaise gets too thick, add more lemon juice or a little hot water. If it starts to curdle, a teaspoon of hot water and hard beating usually sorts it out, or put another egg yolk into a bowl and mix your curdled sauce into it drop by drop.

You can also use vinegar instead of lemon juice, or both. I sometimes put a little mustard into my mayonnaise.

SALSA DE TOMATE
Tomato Sauce
Nationwide

I don't always make this sauce with garlic, depending on what it is being used for. If you are in a hurry, chopped tinned tomatoes can be used instead of fresh.

Makes 500 ml (18 fl. oz)

100 ml (3½ fl. oz) olive oil
2 cloves of garlic, peeled and roughly
chopped
1 medium onion, peeled and chopped
15 g (½ oz) plain flour
1 kg (2¼ lb) tomatoes, skinned, seeded and
chopped
1 bay leaf
5 ml (1 tsp) sugar
salt and pepper

Heat the oil in a saucepan or frying pan. Sauté the garlic and onion gently until transparent, about 10 minutes.

Stir in the flour and cook for about a minute then add the tomatoes, bay leaf, sugar and salt and pepper. Mix well, cover and cook gently for about half an hour, stirring occasionally with a wooden spoon so the sauce doesn't stick.

Remove the bay leaf and either put through a mouli or sieve or blend in a liquidizer. Put back into a saucepan and adjust the consistency. If it is too thick, add a little water; and if it is too liquid, boil quickly for a few minutes without a lid. Adjust seasoning and it is ready.

THE ESSENTIAL SPANISH SAUCES: *MAHONESA/*
MAYONNAISE, *ALLIOLI/*GARLIC SAUCE AND *SALSA DE*
*TOMATE/*TOMATO SAUCE

ALLIOLI
Garlic Sauce
Catalonia

The name of this sauce means literally garlic (*all*) and oil (*oli*) in the Catalan language. In Castilian it is usually written *alioli*. Proper *alioli* is made in a mortar. I give the recipe for true garlic fans as well as a milder one for others. It is eaten with grilled shellfish and fish, some grilled meats and vegetables, and with bread as a *tapa* in many bars.

Makes 250 ml (8 fl. oz)
4 cloves of garlic, peeled and minced
approx. 5 ml (1 tsp) salt
250 ml (8 fl. oz) olive oil

Crush the garlic in a mortar with salt until it becomes a pulp then gradually beat in the oil. The result should be a sort of pale, thick mayonnaise.

The milder sort is made exactly like mayonnaise (see the previous recipe): simply crush the garlic with the lemon juice and egg yolk and then add the salt and oil.

SALMOREJO
Cold Tomato Sauce
Andalusia

This cold sauce is typical of Jaen and Cordoba and goes extremely well with fish. It couldn't be easier to make.

Makes about 300 ml (10 fl. oz.)
50 g (2 oz) fresh breadcrumbs soaked in a
little water
1 clove of garlic, peeled
500 g (18 oz) red tomatoes, skinned
5 ml (1 tsp) salt
65 ml (2½ fl. oz) olive oil
15 ml (1 tbsp) mild white wine vinegar

Put the breadcrumbs, garlic, tomatoes and salt into a mixer. Blend for a few minutes. Add the oil little by little and finally the vinegar. Serve well chilled.

S O P A S · S O U P S

When talking about soups in Spain it is hard to know where to begin, as from north to south and east to west, there is the most tremendous variety. There are soups that are practically meals in themselves or indeed are, such as those made from lentils, beans and chickpeas (also excellent puréed if any is left over from the original dish). Then there are the fish soups of the north, east and south, all so different from each other. Some have become well-known, like the Basque *porrusalda*, and are eaten in many parts of the country. The most famous of all, though, and one dish which has travelled far, is *gazpacho*. This is one of the mainstays of Spanish cuisine, and not surprisingly so as it is refreshing, nourishing and inexpensive. It is interesting that in his book on Andalusian cooking, José Carlos Capél gives some *sixty* recipes for *gazpacho*, and just about every Spanish housewife will boast of having her own unique version. (It gets more confusing. *Gazpacho Manchego* bears little or no resemblance to what most people's idea is of *gazpacho*, as it is a stew made from different varieties of game eaten on a special, round sort of unleavened bread.)

Each region has its own pot-au-feu type dish, which can be a complete meal or just a soup (see introduction to *Carne y Aves*). However, I think Cervantes' description from *Don Quixote* gives a wonderful idea of what might go into an *olla*, as the soup-stew cooking pot is called in La Mancha.

'In a place of La Mancha, whose name I do not remember, there lived not long ago one of those gentlemen who boasts a wooden lance and an old buckler, a scraggy horse and a greyhound for coursing. An *olla* stew containing more cow's meat than mutton, scratch fare most nights . . . lentils on Fridays and perhaps a pigeon on Sundays consumed three-quarters of his substance . . .'

BASIC INGREDIENTS FOR SPANISH SOUPS

THE MOLINO DE GREGORIO PRETO IN VALDEPEÑAS.

GAZPACHO
Andalusia

Most people have eaten this delicious tomato-based soup in one form or another, either in Spain or elsewhere. It has become one of the best-known Spanish dishes abroad. However, even in Spain it is made in so many different ways that one never really knows which is the true *gazpacho* recipe. Some people add less tomato and more water and paprika (a killer on the stomach); others like it thicker or thinner; in some parts of Spain almonds are added, or grapes. However, the soup, which originated in Andalusia, was really a complete meal, perfect for the summer and hot weather; it was easy to digest, but at the same time nourishing. The Andalusian *gazpacho* is often fairly liquid and has diced tomatoes, peppers, cucumber, onion, hard-boiled egg and bread added to taste (as left).

The one I most enjoy is a slightly thicker version with lots of tomatoes and not too much garlic, and the recipe was in fact given to me by a friend from Seville.

Serves 6–8

2 slices of stale bread
2 kg (4 lb, 7 oz) tomatoes, washed and
roughly chopped
1 cucumber, peeled and chopped
1 green pepper, seeded and chopped
1 small onion, peeled and chopped
2 cloves of garlic, peeled and chopped
75 ml (5 tbsp) olive oil
15–30 ml (1–2 tbsp) good wine vinegar to
taste
5 ml (1 tsp) cumin seeds or powder
salt

The bread, although typical, can be left out in this recipe as there is a large quantity of tomatoes. If you wish to use it, soak the bread in a little water, and squeeze it out before using. The bread also helps to thicken the soup and give it a nice consistency.

Blend all the vegetables and the garlic in a mixer, and push through a sieve into a bowl. Use the mixer again to beat the bread, oil and vinegar together. Add some of the tomato, the cumin seeds and salt to taste. Add a little water and mix into the bowl with the soup. Add a few ice cubes and leave to become cold. You can add more water if necessary.

Traditionally the soup was made by crushing the ingredients with a pestle in a mortar and then adding cold water. *Gazpacho* should be served in wooden bowls and eaten with a wooden spoon, although it isn't always! Make large quantities of *gazpacho* as it keeps well – but it won't last long, as you are bound to keep sipping it.

GAZPACHO

SOPA DE ALMENDRAS
Almond Soup
Castile and Andalusia

A soup eaten traditionally at Christmas time, mainly in Castile and Andalusia. It is unusual and delicious, as well as very simple to make.

Serves 4

200 g (7 oz) almonds
1 clove of garlic, peeled
15 ml (1 tbsp) finely chopped parsley
8 slices of stale bread, preferably brown
85 ml (3 fl. oz) olive oil
5 ml (1 tsp) ground cumin
3 ml (½ tsp) saffron
1 litre (1¾ pints) good chicken stock
250 ml (8 fl. oz) milk
salt and pepper

Fry the almonds, garlic, parsley and four slices of the bread in about 60 ml (4 tbsp) of the oil. When golden, put the contents of the pan in a processor and liquidize with the cumin, saffron and a little of the stock. Put in a saucepan, pour in the remaining stock and the milk, season with salt and pepper, and bring to the boil. Lower the heat and cook slowly for about 15 minutes.

Meanwhile, fry the remaining bread slices in the remaining olive oil until golden and crisp.

Bring the soup to the boil again and add the four slices of fried bread. Cover, remove from the stove, and leave for 5 minutes before serving.

THE WINE TOWN OF AGUILAR DE LA FRONTERA IN CORDOBA, ANDALUSIA, WHERE *MONTILLA* IS MADE.

SOPA DE AJO
Garlic Soup
Madrid

This incredibly simple soup is eaten all over Spain, but naturally the recipe varies slightly from region to region. Believe it or not, it used to be served in the wee-small-hours of the morning after late-night parties or a night on the town, whilst the shepherds and farmers were tucking into it for breakfast in the country! However, I'm sure you'll enjoy it more at either lunch or dinner.

Serves 4

30 ml (2 tbsp) olive oil
4 cloves of garlic, peeled and halved
5 ml (1 tsp) paprika
4 slices of French-style bread
1 litre (1¾ pints) water or stock
salt
4 eggs

Heat the oil in a shallow flameproof earthenware casserole or baking dish. Add the garlic halves and cook gently until they are golden. Put them to one side. Lower the heat and add the paprika to the pan. Stir well then add the bread and fry gently for 2–3 minutes. Pour over the cold water or stock (water is traditional, stock would be an improvement), and season with salt. Return the garlic to the pan and cook for 5–6 minutes longer.

Crack the eggs into the soup and place the whole dish in a fairly hot oven – 200°C (400°F) Gas Gas 6 – and bake until the eggs are just set, about 5–7 minutes. Don't overcook, as half the fun is to break the yolk with your spoon and mix it into the soup.

Some people add beaten egg to the soup just before serving, in which case use only 2 eggs. You can also fry the garlic and bread in a frying pan and then divide it between individual baking dishes.

THE SILHOUETTED FIGURES OF CERVANTES' DON QUIXOTE AND HIS HORSE ROSINANTE ON A WALL IN LA MANCHA.

THE *CABALLO ROJA* IN CORDOBA'S JEWISH QUARTER, ONE OF THE CITY'S MOST FAMOUS RESTAURANTS.

SOPA DE ZANAHORIAS A LA MADRILEÑA
Carrot Soup
Madrid

It is fairly unusual to find carrot soup in Spain, but the cook at my father-in-law's house used to make this one which is simple and very good.

Serves 4

50 g (2 oz) butter
1 large onion, peeled and chopped
500 g (18 oz) ripe tomatoes, skinned,
seeded and chopped
15 ml (1 tbsp) chopped parsley
50 ml (2 fl. oz) white wine
1 litre (1¾ pints) vegetable stock
6 large carrots, scraped and chopped
salt
croûtons of fried bread

Melt the butter in a saucepan and sauté the chopped onion. When it is half done add the tomatoes and half the parsley. When the tomato is done (about 5 minutes), add the wine and reduce for a minute or two. Add the stock and carrots and cook for about 45 minutes.

About 10 minutes before serving you can add more stock and some salt if necessary. Serve in a soup tureen, sprinkled with the remaining parsley, and with the fried croûtons passed separately.

CALDO SERRANO
Ham Broth
Cordoba

This simple broth gets its name from *jamon* (ham) *serrano*, the *serrano* coming from the *sierra* or mountains, where the best hams are cured. In Andalusia, some of the best ham comes from Jabugo in the province of Huelva – the so-called *pata negra* or black leg coming from the black Iberian pig of this area – or Trevelez in Granada. On a cold day, a plain *caldo* really warms one up.

Serves 4–6

a large ham bone, preferably serrano
3 litres (5¼ pints) water
2 carrots, trimmed and chopped
1 onion, peeled and chopped
salt

OPTIONAL GARNISH
100 g (4 oz) ham, chopped
1 hard-boiled egg
100 g (4 oz) boiled rice

In a large saucepan or pot, put the ham bone, water, carrots and onion. Bring to the boil and then simmer to allow it to reduce by about half. This will take about 2½ hours. Strain.

Season with salt, then add diced ham, chopped egg and rice if you wish. Serve hot.

CALDO SERRANO/HAM BROTH

POTAJE DE BERROS
Watercress Soup
Canary Islands

This is a very nourishing soup, in fact almost a meal in itself, especially if you eat it as they do in the Fortunate Isles with fresh cheese and *gofio*. This is made from toasted corn, barley or wheat flour and water, and small pieces are eaten with many dishes.

Serves 6

> 300 g (11 oz) dried white beans
> at least 2 litres (3½ pints) water
> 6 bunches of watercress, washed and
> chopped
> 450 g (1 lb) lean pork in one piece
> 150 g (5 oz) lean bacon in one piece
> 2 medium onions, peeled and chopped
> 3 medium tomatoes, skinned, seeded and
> chopped
> 1 kg (2¼ lb) potatoes, peeled and sliced
> 1 clove of garlic, peeled and chopped
> a pinch each of ground cumin, saffron and
> paprika
> 60 ml (4 tbsp) olive oil
> salt and pepper

Soak the beans in cold water overnight, then drain, wash and bring to the boil in a large covered pan in 1.5 litres (2½ pints) of the water. When the water starts to boil, add the remaining cold water and the watercress. Turn the heat down and cook for about 45 minutes.

Add the pork, bacon, onions, tomatoes and potatoes. Cook slowly for another 45 minutes.

Mix the garlic and spices into the oil, and add to the soup. Boil for another 10 minutes. Taste for seasoning.

Before serving allow soup to stand for another 10 minutes off the stove. Cut the meat into slices, place in a tureen and pour the soup over the meats.

SOPA MALLORQUINA
Cabbage Soup
Majorca

The Balearic Islands are well-known for three culinary specialities: *mayonnaise*, which came from the city of Mahon in Menorca; *sobrasada*, the Majorcan red sausage, which is good spread on bread or inside the other speciality from Majorca, the *ensaimada*, a sort of sweet bun. This very thick soup, though not so well-known, is equally good.

Serves 4

> 60 ml (4 tbsp) olive oil
> 4 cloves of garlic, peeled and chopped
> 4 large onions, peeled and chopped
> 2 tomatoes, skinned and chopped
> 15 ml (1 tbsp) chopped parsley
> 1 medium cabbage, chopped
> salt
> 5 ml (1 tsp) paprika
> 400 g (14 oz) brown bread, slightly stale,
> cut into thin rounds

Heat the oil in a casserole or earthenware pot, add the garlic and onions, and sauté until transparent. Add the tomatoes and chopped parsley then the cabbage. When you have mixed it all together season well and add the paprika. Cover with boiling water and cook slowly until the cabbage is done,

about 15–20 minutes.

Remove the vegetables and add the bread to the casserole. Return the vegetables and bring to the boil. Remove from the stove. Leave for 5–10 minutes and then serve from the casserole.

INSIDE THE GREAT MEZQUITA MOSQUE IN THE CITY OF CORDOBA IN THE AREA OF SPAIN WHERE THE BEST HAMS ARE CURED.

POTAJE DE GARBANZOS
Chickpea Soup
Andalusia

This soup was a regular feature of Friday Lent menus in the old days when no good Catholic was supposed to eat meat. It is also very popular in the winter, almost a meal in itself. This recipe is typical of Madrid.

Serves 6

500 g (18 oz) chickpeas
salt
250 g (9 oz) dried salt cod
2.5 litres (4½ pints) water
1 bay leaf
250 g (9 oz) potatoes, peeled and finely chopped
500 g (18 oz) spinach, washed, destalked and drained
2 cloves of garlic, peeled
2 sprigs of parsley, chopped
5 ml (1 tsp) ground cumin
a pinch of paprika
1 large onion, peeled and chopped
45 ml (3 tbsp) olive oil
7.5 ml (½ tbsp) plain flour
1 hard-boiled egg, finely chopped

Soak the chickpeas the night before in plenty of warm water with a pinch of salt. The dried salt cod must also be soaked in cold water and the water should be changed at least once.

Put the chickpeas in a large saucepan with the measured water and the bay leaf. Bring to the boil and cook for about 1½ hours – the time depends on the type of chickpea. Add the cod after 45 minutes.

When the chickpeas are nearly cooked, add the potatoes and spinach. Cook for about 5 minutes.

Meanwhile in a mortar crush the garlic with the parsley, cumin and a little paprika. Mix it all together in the mortar with a spoonful of the soup. Gently fry the chopped onion in the oil, then stir in the flour and the contents of the mortar. Cook for a minute or two, then add to the chickpeas.

Test for salt, and remove the bay leaf. Serve in a tureen sprinkled with chopped hard-boiled egg.

*POTAJE DE GARBANZOS/*CHICKPEA SOUP

PORRUSALDA
Leek, Potato and Cod Soup
Basque Country

This soup from the Basque Country is made basically from leeks and potatoes. The addition of dried salt cod gives it a special flavour, and makes it that bit different. (If you can't get salt cod, you could substitute smoked haddock.) Be careful with the seasoning because if the cod is salty you'll need very little. If you want to add pepper and a bay leaf, go ahead. It may not be traditional, but I like it.

Serves 4–6

250 g (9 oz) dried salt cod
1.5 litres (2½ pints) light stock (you can use
a stock cube) or water
2–3 cloves of garlic, peeled
15 ml (1 tbsp) olive oil
6 fat leeks, washed and cut into 2.5 cm (1
in) pieces
750 g (a good 1½ lb) potatoes, peeled and
thickly sliced
1 bay leaf
salt

Soak the cod in cold water overnight. Change the water once or more, depending on how salty the cod is.

Drain and dry cod. Place in a saucepan and cover with the cold stock or water. Bring to the boil, remove cod and keep the water. Flake the cod into large pieces.

Sauté the garlic in the oil in a saucepan until golden. Add the leeks and sauté for a minute or two, then add the potatoes. Stir well with a wooden spoon and add the pieces of cod.

Cover with the stock you boiled the cod in and add the bay leaf. Put lid on and cook slowly for about 45 minutes or until the leeks and potatoes are done. Adjust seasoning before serving, and remove bay leaf and garlic.

SOPA DE PESCADO CON FIDEOS
Fish Soup with Noodles
Barcelona

This is one of the many excellent fish soups that come from Catalonia. It is easy to make but does require long, slow cooking. The effort is worth it, though, and it's very economical too!

Serves 6

1 onion, peeled and chopped
60 ml (4 tbsp) olive oil
30 ml (2 tbsp) plain flour
250 g (9 oz) eel or angler (monk) fish, cut
in pieces
1 angler (monk) fish head
3 tomatoes, halved
1 bay leaf
2 sprigs of parsley
2.5 litres (4½ pints) water
salt and pepper
2 carrots, scraped and chopped
4 cloves of garlic, peeled
a pinch of saffron
10 almonds and hazelnuts, roasted and
roughly chopped
200 g (7 oz) noodles or spaghetti
grated Gruyère cheese

In a large saucepan sauté the chopped onion in the oil. When it is golden, stir in the flour, and stir together to blend. Add the fish and the fish head, the tomatoes, bay leaf, parsley and the water. Season with salt and pepper and bring to the boil. Cook slowly for 1½ hours.

Next add the carrots, the garlic, saffron and nuts and cook for another hour or a little more.

Remove the fish head and strain the soup through a sieve, pressing well to extract all the juices. Now boil the liquid you have obtained and add the noodles, which you've broken into pieces. When the noodles are done, add the pieces of fish from the head to the soap. Serve in a tureen and sprinkle well with grated cheese, or serve separately if you wish.

SOPA DE PICADILLO
Leftover Soup
Nationwide

Different versions of this quick soup from leftovers can be found nearly all over Spain. If, for example, you haven't got one of the ingredients such as the ham, you could add a chicken liver. It is equally good.

Serves 4

1 breast of a boiling fowl or chicken,
cooked
100 g (4 oz) ham
1 hard-boiled egg
about 1 litre (1¾ pints) good meat or
chicken stock
100 ml (3½ fl. oz) white wine or sherry
salt and pepper

If you have a cooked chicken breast left over, chop it finely. Do the same with the ham. Add the mashed egg yolk and the chopped white. Pour over sufficient stock, add the wine and adjust the seasoning.

You could also make the stock by cooking a raw chicken breast with onion, carrot, bay leaf, parsley, seasoning and sufficient water. You could of course use a stock cube.

SOPA DE PESCADO CON MAHONESA
Fish Soup with Mayonnaise
Andalusia

When I first ate this soup – made by the mother of a friend of mine from Granada – I thought it was simply delicious. The mayonnaise makes it a wonderfully creamy consistency, and gives that special touch to an extremely simple dish. All you really need is a good fish stock to be sure of success.

Serves 6

500 g (18 oz) any white fish (hake, cod etc)
1.5 litres (2½ pints) good fish stock
45 ml (3 tbsp) mayonnaise (see page 60)
salt and pepper

Wash the fish well and cut it into small pieces. Boil it in a little of the stock. Remove the fish when it is cooked, a few minutes. Add the hot stock, drop by drop, to the mayonnaise in a saucepan. Mix well. Add the remainder of the stock, and bring to the boil. Add the fish, season and there you are.

There is no reason why you shouldn't garnish with croûtons, parsley or even hard-boiled egg.

CALDO DE PERRO GADITANO
Fish Broth
Cadiz

This is a really simple and tasty fish soup, from the old port of Andalusia, the addition of orange juice giving it a special flavour. The name is curious, too, as it literally means 'dog's broth Cadiz style'!

Serves 4

> *1 kg (2¼ lb) whiting or white fish*
> *salt*
> *2 cloves of garlic, peeled*
> *75 ml (5 tbsp) olive oil*
> *1 onion, peeled and finely chopped*
> *1 litre (1¾ pints) boiling water*
> *juice of 2 bitter oranges*

Prepare the fish and cut it into thick slices. Sprinkle with salt and leave for an hour.

Fry the garlic in the oil in a casserole, remove when it is golden, and add the finely chopped onion. Cook for a minute until transparent, then add the boiling water.

Cover casserole and allow the onion to cook well, about 5–10 minutes. Add the fish, more water if necessary and cook for 15 minutes. Remove from the stove, add the orange juice, and adjust salt.

Serve hot. Some people like to put slices of white bread into their soup.

SOPA DE PATATA RALLADA
Grated Potato Soup
Madrid

Like the leftover soup, this is quick to make as well, basically if you have some good stock left over. You can use as much potato as you like, depending on how thick you like your soup.

Serves 2

> *500 ml (18 fl. oz) good meat or chicken stock*
> *1 medium potato, peeled*
> *salt and pepper*
> *15 ml (1 tbsp) chopped parsley*

Bring the stock to the boil, and grate the potato into it. Cook for a few minutes. Adjust seasoning, and serve with a sprinkling of chopped parsley on top.

A CAMEL PLOUGH IN USE BY A FARMER IN LANZAROTE, IN THE CANARY ISLANDS, WHERE THE DELICATE WATERCRESS SOUP ORIGINATES. (PHOTO BY IMAGE BANK)

AGRICULTURAL LANDSCAPE OF THE LA MANCHA REGION.

·PESCADOS Y MARISCOS·
FISH AND SHELLFISH

Spain is a paradise for fish lovers, but don't imagine that you have to be beside the sea to get the best. In inland places, there will be marvellous fish dishes on offer, although there is usually some other speciality one wants to try. Madrid, however, is the exception. Fish dishes are very special there, and *Madrileños* are known as *gatos* (cats) because of their love of fish! In the old days the fish was brought fresh to Madrid from the northern ports overnight in refrigerated lorries; the town of Aranda de Duero is well known for its excellent dishes of fresh cod because it was the half-way stop for the lorries on their way to the city. (I was told this by Seri, the brilliant owner of *El Mesón de la Villa*, who makes many other good fish dishes using trout from the River Duero and dried cod which needs no refrigeration.)

I have tried to choose a selection of some of the simpler dishes because, although the ingredients are not complicated, some of the Basque hake dishes require a lot of patience and expertise to make them. The classic *al pil-pil*

sauce, for instance, made from oil, garlic and dried red peppers, sounds simple enough. But, after the fish, either dried cod or hake, is fried gently, an emulsion is supposed to form by gently shaking the pan. This is much less easy to achieve.

A visit to a market in any of the major cities – San Miguel in Madrid or the one in Las Ramblas in Barcelona, in particular – is a real treat, the variety of fish and shellfish making a most colourful and appetizing display. In Barcelona the dried cod can be bought in any of its different stages of de-salting. It is displayed in water or dry, and you only have to explain what you want and your requirements will be met.

FISH AND SHELLFISH COMMONLY USED IN SPANISH COOKING, INCLUDING A TAIL OF HAKE, RED MULLET, SQUID AND WHITE ANGLER (MONK) FISH

BACALAO A LA VIZCAINA
Dried Salt Cod with Red Peppers
Basque Country

Although fresh fish is plentiful in the north of Spain, curiously enough dried salt cod is the basis of many Basque dishes. For this recipe dried, sweet red peppers called *pimientos choriceros* are used, but if you use fresh or tinned ones you'll get good results even though it won't be so authentic. This dish improves if made a day in advance and reheated.

Serves 4

> 800 g (1¾ lb) dried salt cod, cut into
> rectangles of about 8 × 6 cm (3¼ × 2½ in)
> 8 dried red peppers
> 90 g (3½ oz) lard
> 3 onions, peeled and finely chopped

Soak the cod overnight in water, changing the water once or twice. Soak the peppers in water overnight as well.

In a fireproof casserole heat the lard and gently cook the onion until extremely soft, virtually dissolving. (Gently really means gently, and Basque cookery books recommend about 3 hours.) Add a little water if the mass of onion gets too thick. Skin the peppers and cook with the onion for about an hour of the cooking time. Put the whole lot through a sieve or mouli.

Drain the cod and place the pieces skin up into into the casserole and pour the onion and pepper purée over them. Simmer until the fish is cooked – about 20–30 minutes – either on top of the cooker or in a moderate oven.

Many people use hard-boiled egg yolks and toasted breadcrumbs to thicken the sauce which is also good.

BESUGO AL HORNO
Baked Sea Bream
Madrid

Sea bream used to be traditional Christmas fare in many parts of Spain, but as prices more than double at that time of year, not everybody can afford it. It is such a good fish that there are several restaurants in Madrid that specialize in it. My sister who came to stay from England, where she found the fish pretty boring, became really 'hooked' on *besugo*.

Get your fishmonger to clean it and make three or four slits crosswise down the back. You can have the eyes removed or not – the old Spanish nanny who looked after my oldest son always said they were a great delicacy!

Serves 4

> 1 whole sea bream, about 1.5 kg (3 lb, 5 oz)
> in weight
> salt
> 1 onion, peeled and sliced
> 2 tomatoes, washed and sliced
> 1 lemon, washed and sliced
> a sprig of parsley
> 150 ml (5 fl. oz) olive oil
> 4 medium potatoes, peeled and thinly
> sliced

Wash the fish then sprinkle with salt inside and out. Preheat the oven to about 200°C (400°F) Gas 6. Put the fish in a large oval ovenproof dish. Cut two slices of the onion in half and fit them into one of the slits in the fish; do the same with two slices of the tomato and the lemon in the other slits. Put some lemon inside the fish and some parsley and you can put a round of lemon in the eye. Pour the oil over the fish. Arrange the potato slices around the dish and any remaining slices of onion and tomato. Season and put in the oven.

Bake for about 20–25 minutes. If the fish is large I sometimes cover the top with a piece of foil for about 15 minutes of the cooking time. Baste occasionally. If you are not going to serve immediately turn off the oven before the fish has finished cooking and leave it. It will be done but not overcooked.

A FISH EATER AT HOME IN SAN ESTEBAN.

VINEYARDS IN THE COOL NORTHERN REGION OF NAVARRA.

BONITO CON TOMATE
Bonito with Tomato
Basque Country

One of the tunny fish family, bonito is plentiful in midsummer along the Cantabrian coast. In this recipe I have used a kilo (2¼ lb) of bonito for four although, depending on how much you eat, about 150 g (5 oz) per person is usually sufficient as it is a filling fish. I like to make more, as it keeps and re-heats well.

Serves 4

> 1 kg (2¼ lb) bonito, in a thick slice
> salt
> 20 g (¾ oz) plain flour
> 150 ml (5 fl. oz) olive oil
> 1.5 kg (3 lb, 5 oz) ripe tomatoes, skinned,
> seeded and chopped
> 1 bay leaf
> 5 ml (1 tsp) sugar
> 1 large clove of garlic, peeled and finely
> chopped
> 5 ml (1 tsp) finely chopped parsley

Remove the black skin from the fish and cut the flesh into chunks. In Spain the fishmonger will do this. Wash the fish, dry well, season with salt and dip in flour. Heat the oil in a frying pan and fry the fish on all sides. Place the pieces in an ovenproof dish. Preheat the oven to 180–190°C (350–375°F) Gas 4–5.

In the same frying pan fry the tomatoes for about 10 minutes, then add the bay leaf, the sugar and 5 ml (1 tsp) salt. Cook for about 5 minutes longer without a lid to reduce the sauce. Pour this over the fish (which it should cover), and sprinkle on the garlic and parsley. Put in the oven and bake for about 15 minutes.

As not everybody is mad about garlic I have frequently made this dish without it, and it is still very good.

BONITO CON NATA
Bonito Baked in Cream
Asturias

This recipe can also be made with tunny fish. It was given to me by my son Alfonso, who learned how to make this simple and delicious dish in Asturias. It is definitely not for weight-watchers, although I think it is worth making an exception to try it.

Serves 4

> 750 g (a good 1½ lb) fresh bonito, cut into
> slices about 2.5cm (1 in) thick
> salt and pepper
> 30 g (1¼ oz) butter
> 1 litre (1¾ pints) double cream

Preheat the oven to 200°C (400°F) Gas 6. Wash and dry the fish, and season with salt and pepper. Generously grease an earthenware casserole or ovenproof dish with the butter, then place the fish in the dish.

Pour the cream over the fish (which it should cover), and bake in the oven for about 15 minutes. If your oven is too hot turn it down slightly after 5 minutes.

BONITO CON NATA/BONITO BAKED IN CREAM

MARMITAKO
Tunny Fish Stew
Basque Country

Tradition has it that the Basque fishermen had to provide their own bread for lunch to accompany the freshly caught fish, and the shipowner would provide the wine! Lunch is called *ameiketako* in Basque, which is where the name *marmitako* comes from. Nowadays the dish is always made from tunny fish or bonito, but there is no doubt that the primitive versions of the recipe were made from whatever the catch brought in. This fish stew was also made before the potato was known in Europe, so it is more than likely that the crew's version only included fish, some sort of fat, and bread which was probably pretty stale after days at sea. Later on, potatoes and dried peppers would have been added, but perishable tomatoes would not.

Serves 4

> 750 g (a good 1½ lb) tunny fish
> salt and pepper
> 100 ml (3½ fl. oz) olive oil
> 1 onion, peeled and cut into rings
> 1 green pepper, seeded and cut into rounds
> 3 tomatoes, skinned, seeded and chopped
> (optional)
> 2 cloves of garlic, peeled and chopped
> 5 ml (1 tsp) chopped parsley
> 1 kg (2¼ lb) potatoes, peeled and quartered
> about 1 litre (1¾ pints) hot water
> 1 bay leaf
> 100 g (4 oz) bread cut in thin slices
> (optional)

Wash the fish and cut into squares. Season with salt and keep to one side.

Heat the oil in an flameproof earthenware pot or thick casserole and sauté the onion and pepper. When the onion is transparent, add the tomatoes if you are using them. Continue to cook for 5 minutes. Meanwhile crush the garlic and parsley together, then add to the pan plus the potatoes. Mix well together, cover with hot water, add the bay leaf and season well. Bring to the boil and cook until the potatoes are almost done. Add more water if necessary. There shouldn't be too much liquid.

Add the fish, cover and cook for a minute or two. Remove from the heat and leave for about 10 minutes before serving. Add the bread then if you wish.

MERLUZA A LA SIDRA
Hake in Cider
Asturias

Asturias is the Spanish area for apples and cider, so it is not surprising that cider is used in the cooking. The best is the draught cider which has to be poured in a special way to give it a little fizz. The bottle is held shoulder high and the cider poured into a big glass, but only the amount you can drink in one gulp as otherwise it becomes completely flat. Any that you haven't drunk you throw away and start again!

Serves 4

> 6 potatoes, peeled and sliced
> 6 slices hake, approx. 150 g (5 oz) each
> salt
> 150 ml (5 fl. oz) olive oil
> 3 cloves of garlic, peeled and chopped

5 ml (1 tsp) paprika
1 bay leaf
250 ml (8 fl. oz) cider

Wash the potatoes and fish. Dry well and season with salt.

Heat the oil in a large pan and add the potatoes and garlic. Sauté until they begin to turn golden then pour off any excess oil. Add the paprika, bay leaf and the cider. Bring to the boil and allow to cook for a few minutes.

Add the slices of hake, cover, and cook gently for about 15 minutes. If there is too little liquid add more cider. Remove the bay leaf, arrange on a serving dish and eat hot.

MERLUZA A LA VASCA
Hake with Asparagus
Basque Country

This Basque recipe is popular all over Spain, as Spaniards are great fish eaters. Of course the fresher the fish the better the dish, but it can also be made with frozen hake. You'd be surprised to hear true gourmets discussing for hours where the best hake comes from and how it was caught. The most appreciated are those caught on a hook and line apparently!

Serves 6
6 thick slices of hake, about 200 g (7 oz)
each
500 g (18 oz) fresh peas, podded, or a 125 g
(4½ oz) can
a bunch of fresh asparagus, the thin stems
(failing this, a tin of asparagus tips)

60 ml (4 tbsp) olive oil
1 medium onion, peeled and chopped
1 clove of garlic, peeled and chopped
15 ml (1 tbsp) plain flour
approx. 200 ml (7 fl. oz) water
salt
1 sprig of parsley
15 ml (1 tbsp) chopped parsley
1 hard-boiled egg, chopped

Cook the peas and asparagus in the normal way, and keep warm. If you are using tins, open and drain them.

For the sauce, heat the oil in a frying pan, and gently fry the onion and garlic until transparent, about 6 minutes. Stir in the flour then add 100 ml (3½ fl. oz) cold water. Stir continuously with a wooden spoon for about 8 minutes.

Place the slices of fish, which you have salted, in a large flameproof dish; be sure there is plenty of room – one of the big round clay ones is ideal. Put the sauce through a mouli and pour over the fish; add another 100 ml (3½ fl. oz) water if necessary so that the fish is just covered. Add the sprig of parsley and cook over a slow flame, shaking the dish occasionally so that the fish doesn't stick, but taking care that it doesn't break up. This will take about 15 minutes.

Just before serving remove the sprig of parsley then garnish with the chopped parsley. Arrange the peas and asparagus tips around the dish and sprinkle on the chopped egg. Adjust seasoning, heat gently and serve immediately.

COLA DE MERLUZA A LO MARICHU
Hake with Wine and Hazelnuts
Basque Country

This excellent recipe came from a book published in Franco's time by the '*Sección femenina*', the Phalangist Women's Movement. All girls had to do the equivalent of military service which naturally included cooking. Luckily I didn't have to do it, but I did find the book very useful although a bit difficult to follow at first as my Spanish was not up to many of the cookery terms and vocabulary.

Serves 6

1.5 kg (3 lb, 5 oz) hake, a piece cut from the
tail end
the hake's head
½ onion, peeled and thickly sliced
1 carrot, scrubbed and roughly chopped
300 ml (10 fl. oz) white wine
150 ml (5 fl. oz) water
salt and pepper
7 or 8 hazelnuts, peeled and roasted
½ clove of garlic, peeled
a pinch of coarse salt
2 eggs, hard-boiled
2 slices of fried bread, chopped
5 ml (1 tsp) chopped parsley

Wash and scale the fish, if your fishmonger has not done so. Put it in a flameproof oval or rectangular dish, and add the fish head, the onion and carrot. Pour over the wine and water, season with salt and freshly ground black pepper, and bring to the boil. Remove any froth and cook for 5 minutes. Pour off the liquid you have cooked the fish in and reduce it by boiling for about 10 minutes. Meanwhile keep the fish warm and covered, off the heat.

Remove the fish head, and liquidize the contents of the dish. Crush the hazelnuts, garlic and coarse salt in a mortar (or a processor), then add the two egg yolks, fried bread and parsley. Add some of the stock to the mortar, mix well then add to the rest of the stock. Pour the sauce over the fish and heat together for a few minutes before serving.

MENDING THE NETS IN THE FISHING VILLAGE OF BONANZA IN ANDALUSIA. (PHOTO BY ADAM WOOLFITT, SUSAN GRIGGS AGENCY)

COLA DE MERLUZA A LO MARICHU/HAKE WITH WINE AND HAZELNUTS

(*OVERLEAF*) TROUT RIVER AT THE SMALL TOWN OF ESTELLA IN NAVARRA.

RAPE EN ADOBO
Marinated Fried Angler (Monk) Fish
Granada

This delicious dish can be made with any firm fish. In Andalusia, particularly in Seville, one of my favourite *tapas* is *cazon*, a fish from the shark family which is marinated and fried just like the recipe below. (In the case of *cazon*, unless you marinate it, the fish is pretty tasteless.) A Portuguese friend who is an excellent cook used to marinate the fish in lemon juice and not vinegar.

Serves 4

500 g (18 oz) angler (monk) fish, washed
and cut into small pieces
plain flour for coating
oil for deep-frying

MARINADE
3 cloves of garlic, peeled and crushed
fresh or dried oregano to taste
3 ml (½ tsp) paprika
5 ml (1 tsp) salt
250 ml (8 fl. oz) white wine vinegar
50 ml (2 fl. oz) water

Put the fish in a clay or glass dish. Cover with all the marinade ingredients and mix gently but well. Leave to marinate for at least 2 hours.

Remove the fish and dry it. Dip the pieces of drained fish in flour, and then deep-fry in very hot oil until golden. Serve immediately.

SARDINAS AL OREGANO
Sardines with Oregano
Andalusia

The smaller sardines from the South of Spain are ideal for this excellent dish, which is good as a *tapa*, first course or even a main course if accompanied by a good salad. I like to make quite a large quantity as the sardines keep well. In the summer it is a useful standby if people just drop in.

Serves 4

500 g (18 oz) fresh sardines
150 ml (5 fl. oz) olive oil
2 cloves of garlic, peeled and finely chopped
20 ml (4 tsp) chopped oregano
salt and pepper
200 ml (7 fl. oz) wine vinegar
200 ml (7 fl. oz) water

Wash and clean the sardines, and cut off their heads. Heat the oil in a large frying pan and fry them for a few minutes on each side. Arrange them in a fire-proof clay dish and pour over a little of the oil you have fried them in.

Mix the garlic, oregano, salt and ground black pepper into the vinegar and water. Pour this over the sardines. Bring slowly to the boil and simmer for 5 minutes. Allow to get cold.

The amount of vinegar used is really a matter of taste.

SARDINAS AL OREGANO/SARDINES WITH OREGANO

RAPE CON MIEL
Angler (Monk) Fish in Honey Sauce
Andalusia

Although this is undoubtedly of Arab origin, I first ate it at my local restaurant, *Paulino's*. He loves to experiment, and this less usual regional dish has been greatly appreciated by all his customers.

Serves 4

750 g (a good 1½ lb) angler (monk) fish,
washed and cut in pieces
salt
plain flour for coating
olive oil for frying
10 g (¼ oz) each of pine kernels and
currants

SAUCE
1 onion, peeled and finely chopped
50 ml (2 fl. oz) olive oil
100 ml (3½ fl. oz) honey
juice of 1 lemon
250 ml (8 fl. oz) fish stock (a stock cube
will do)
3 or 4 strands of saffron

For the sauce, sauté the onion very gently in the oil for about 15 minutes until transparent. Add the honey and cook gently until golden. Add the lemon juice and the fish stock, bring to the boil, and cook for about 4 minutes. Add the saffron. Blend the sauce in a liquidizer and then sieve.

Season the fish with salt. Dip the pieces in flour and then fry in hot olive oil in a frying pan, turning once. This seals the fish and prevents it losing its moistness. Remove from the pan and put in a casserole. Cover with the sauce and sprinkle with the pine kernels and currants. Heat gently for about 5 minutes, and it's ready to serve.

Apples sautéed in butter make a nice garnish.

SARDINAS A LA SANTANDERINA
Baked Sardines
Santander

There are innumerable ways of cooking sardines, but this is one of the simplest and least troublesome, especially if you can get your fishmonger to clean them. The fat, juicy sardines in the north of Spain, in Galicia, Asturias and Old Castile, are perfect.

Serve 4–6

1 kg (2¼ lb) fresh sardines
100 ml (3½ fl. oz) olive oil
3 cloves of garlic, peeled and finely chopped
50 g (2 oz) parsley, finely chopped
150 g (5 oz) fine breadcrumbs
salt
4 lemons

Clean the sardines. Remove the heads, scale them, and remove the backbones and the skin (I have to confess that I usually leave the skins on).

Brush the fillets with olive oil and dip in a mixture of the garlic, parsley, breadcrumbs and salt. Place in a single layer in an ovenproof dish and bake in a medium oven – about 180°C (350°F) Gas 4 – for about 15 minutes. (You can put a little extra oil in the pan or dish so that they don't stick.) Serve with wedges of lemon.

TRUCHAS EN ESCABECHE
Marinated Trout
Nationwide

This recipe can be used with many fish but trout and sardines are very good done this way. I find it very useful to have some marinated trout in the refrigerator, and they make a lovely dish accompanied by a salad in the summer.

Serves 4

4 fresh trout
flour for dusting
250 ml (8 fl. oz) olive oil
4 cloves of garlic, peeled
6 cloves
10 black peppercorns
2 bay leaves
1 sprig of thyme
1 sprig of parsley
250 ml (8 fl. oz) dry white wine
250 ml (8 fl. oz) white wine vinegar
100 ml (3½ fl. oz) water
10 ml (2 tsp) salt
a pinch of sugar

Clean and dry the trout. Dust them with flour whilst heating the oil in a frying pan. Fry the trout over a medium heat until golden then remove them from the pan and place in an earthenware or glass dish.

Fry the garlic in the oil in the pan. When it is golden take the pan off the fire and add the cloves, peppercorns, bay leaves, thyme and parsley. Let the oil cool slightly and then add the wine, vinegar, water, salt and sugar. Boil this mixture for a minute and pour it over the fish.

Cover the dish, allow to cool, and then refrigerate for at least 24 hours before eating. Remove bay leaves after a few hours. After 24 hours, test marinade and adjust seasoning according to taste. These trout can be kept for about 2 months in the refrigerator.

ARROZ A BANDA
Seafood with Rice and Potatoes
Levante

A *banda* in Valencian means 'apart', and in this dish which is made in a *paella* pan, the fish and shellfish used to give the rice its flavour are eaten separately. You can use whatever fish is available and add shellfish and squid if you wish. *Alioli* sauce usually accompanies this dish (see page 61).

Serves 4

1 kg (2¼ lb) fish (angler or monk, grouper,
mullet, bream, scorpion-fish)
250 g (9 oz) squid or cuttlefish
150 ml (5 fl. oz) olive oil
2 medium onions, peeled and diced
4 medium potatoes, peeled and halved
a pinch of paprika
salt and pepper
1.5 litres (2½ pints) water
2 cloves of garlic, peeled and chopped
2 medium tomatoes, skinned, seeded and
chopped
350 g (12 oz) short-grain rice
3 ml (½ tsp) powdered saffron

Wash and clean the fish and cut in half if large (depending on variety). Clean the squid, and cut it either into rings or pieces.

Heat 3 tablespoons of olive oil in a *paella* or large saucepan and sauté the onion and potatoes until the potatoes are beginning to turn golden. Sprinkle on the paprika, salt and pepper and add the water quickly so the paprika doesn't burn and give your stock a nasty taste. Bring to the boil, cover, and cook for about 15 minutes until the potatoes are nearly done.

Add the fish, lower the heat and simmer for another 10 minutes. Remove from the heat to another dish and keep covered.

Heat the rest of the oil in your *paella* and sauté the squid, then the garlic and the tomatoes. Stir in the rice, about 1.25 litres (2¼ pints) stock from the fish, and the saffron. Bring to the boil and cook quickly for the first 8–10 minutes and then reduce the heat. Add more stock if necessary. When the rice is cooked let it rest for a few minutes before serving.

The fish is served separately from its dish with the potatoes, and the squid with the rice.

FIDEUA
Noodles and Potatoes with Clams
Levante

Fideuá is basically a dish made in a *paella* from *'fideos'* which are noodles slightly thicker than spaghetti. This recipe includes potatoes as well and you can make it in a large frying pan. If you like things hot, add a chilli pepper when you add the water.

THE PUENTE LA REINA CROSSING THE ARGA RIVER IN NAVARRA.

Serves 4

1 onion, peeled and diced
1 green pepper, seeded and diced
100 ml (3½ fl. oz) olive oil
2 tomatoes, skinned, seeded and chopped
5 ml (1 tsp) paprika
500 g (18 oz) potatoes, peeled and finely sliced
1.25 litres (2¼ pints) water
5 ml (1 tsp) ground black pepper
5 ml (1 tsp) salt
1 clove of garlic, peeled and finely chopped
10 ml (2 tsp) finely chopped parsley
250 g (9 oz) noodles
500 g (18 oz) clams

Sauté the onion and pepper in the oil then, after about 4 minutes, add the tomatoes and paprika. Next add the potatoes and cook until they start to become transparent, then cover with the water.

Mix the pepper, salt, garlic and parsley together with a little of the potato liquid, then add to the pan. Put in the noodles and the clams and cook until the noodles are done, about 7 minutes. Let the dish stand for about 5 minutes before serving.

99

PEZ ESPADA A LA PLANCHA
Grilled Sword Fish
Andalusia

I find sword fish at its best when simply grilled, although it can be equally good dipped in egg and breadcrumbs and then fried. Sauce tartare or mayonnaise is a must with the latter.

Serves 4

> *600 g (1 lb, 5 oz) sword fish, cut into slices*
> *salt*
> *60 ml (4 tbsp) olive oil*
> *2 cloves of garlic, peeled and finely chopped*
> *30 ml (2 tbsp) finely chopped parsley*
> *juice of 1 lemon*

Wash and dry the fish. Season on both sides with salt. Heat the grill.

Put the fish on the grill pan, the sort that has a tray to catch the juices, and pour half the oil over each slice. Next sprinkle a mixture of half the garlic and parsley over the fish. Squeeze over a few drops of lemon juice, and place under a hot grill. When the slices are golden (about 5 minutes) turn over and repeat the operation.

When the fish is cooked serve it in a hot dish and pour over the juices from the pan. It can be served with mayonnaise.

TRUCHAS A LA NAVARRA
Trout with Ham
Navarre

Trout used to be a delicacy but now, thanks to the fish farms, they are found everywhere and are cheap to buy. Do be careful not to overcook your fish as there is nothing worse than a dried-up trout. If you prepare it as below, it will cook through but not dry out.

Serves 4

> *4 medium trout, cleaned, but with their*
> *heads on*
> *salt and pepper*
> *lemon juice*
> *4 thin slices of ham*
> *flour for dusting*
> *60 ml (4 tbsp) olive oil*

Preheat the oven to 190°C (375°F) Gas 5. Just before sautéing the trout, turn the oven *off*.

Season the fish inside and out with salt and pepper and sprinkle with lemon juice. Place a piece of ham inside each trout. Dust with flour. Heat the oil in a large, thick frying pan and sauté the fish quickly on each side, then keep for 10 minutes in the warm, turned-off oven.

Another way is to wrap the ham round the fish which you've seasoned and dusted with flour. Secure it with a wooden toothpick and fry. Remove the toothpick before serving!

Boiled potatoes and slices of lemon are a classic garnish.

THE WINERY OF *CODORNÍU* AT SAN SADURNI DE NOYA IN CATALONIA, WHERE SUPERB WHITE WINES ARE MADE.

ZARZUELA DE PESCADO
Seafood Stew
Catalonia

Typical along the north-east coast, once again there are innumerable ways of making this combination of fish and shellfish. You can use whatever fish you have available, but I think this recipe has a good mixture.

Serves 4

> 500 g (18 oz) squid, cleaned and cut into rings
> 400 g (14 oz) angler (monk) fish, washed and cut into steaks
> 400g (14 oz) hake, washed and cut into steaks
> 500 g (18 oz) mussels, cleaned
> 400 g (14 oz) prawns in shell
> 2 bay leaves
> 3 cloves of garlic, peeled
> a sprig of parsley
> salt and pepper
> 750 ml (1¼ pints) water
> 100 ml (3½ fl. oz) olive oil
> plain flour
> 1 onion, peeled and diced
> 500 g (18 oz) tomatoes, skinned, seeded and chopped
> 5 ml (1 tsp) chopped parsley
> 150 ml (5 fl. oz) dry white wine
> fried croûtons and chopped parsley or chives to serve

If you have cleaned the fish and shellfish yourself, make a light fish stock by putting the bones, heads and fish skin with the mussels in a saucepan with one of the bay leaves, a clove of the garlic, the sprig of parsley and some salt; otherwise just use the mussels and aromatics. Cover with the cold water, bring to the boil, and cook for a minute or two. Strain off the liquid and keep, and remove the mussels from their shells if you like. Discard any that have not opened.

Heat the oil and sauté the remaining garlic and bay leaf for a few minutes. Remove and put to one side. In the same oil lightly fry the fish and squid which you have dipped in flour. Sauté the prawns briefly. Next put the fish and squid in a fireproof dish and arrange the mussels and prawns on top.

In the oil you have fried the fish in, sauté the onion and tomato. Crush the two cooked cloves of garlic with some salt, ground pepper and the chopped parsley, and stir into the tomato and onions. Add the wine and fish stock, cover and cook slowly for about 15 minutes. Put through a mouli and pour over the fish. Cook for about 10 minutes at a low heat, shaking the dish occasionally so the fish doesn't stick. Adjust the seasoning, and serve in the same dish, garnished with croûtons and chopped parsley or chives.

ZARZUELA DE PESCADO/SEAFOOD STEW

·CARNE Y AVES·
MEAT AND POULTRY

In nearly every part of Spain there is some sort of *pot au feu*, a combination of meats, vegetables and beans simmered for a long time in a pot. The one I know best is the *Cocido Madrileño*, which was almost certainly a Jewish dish. When the Jews were expelled from Spain in 1492, the converts to Christianity who remained behind – the Mozarabs – demonstrated their faith by adding pork to it. The chickpea, or *garbanzo*, which is the basis of *cocido*, was probably brought to Spain by the Carthaginians, but it got the name from the Mozarabic word *arbanco*. And *arbancos* or *garbanzos* in one form or another have been boiling away in clay pots all over Spain ever since the fifteenth century. In Galicia, the *Pote Gallego* does not have *garbanzos*, but includes green turnip tips called *grelos*; the Catalan *Escudella i Carn d'Olla* includes the *butifarra* sausage and forcemeat as well as chickpeas. In any part of the country, if you find the words, *pote, puchero, olla* or *potaje* on the menu, go ahead and try them.

I have included *paella* in the main courses, although in Spain it is often eaten as a first course, because it is really worth making it a complete meal with, say, a salad.

I have tried to choose and reproduce recipes from different regions that include many of Spain's best and most characteristic products – among them almonds, tomatoes, olives, red peppers, wine and, naturally, garlic.

COLLECTING THE CROCUS FLOWERS IN LA MANCHA, WHICH PROVIDE THE PRECIOUS SAFFRON, ESSENTIAL INGREDIENT OF *PAELLA*. (PHOTO BY SANTIAGO MUELAS, ASPECT PICTURE LIBRARY)

BASIC INGREDIENTS USED IN COOKING MEAT AND
POULTRY DISHES

PAELLA VALENCIANA/CHICKEN PAELLA

PAELLA VALENCIANA
Chicken Paella
Levante

It was only after many years in Spain that I discovered to my surprise that *paella* is actually the name of the pan in which the rice is cooked. The best rice to use is the short-grain variety which absorbs more liquid. Rice should not be washed, and always keep a little extra stock in case you need to add it. If you use strands of saffron, it is a good idea to toast the saffron by putting it in foil over heat for a few minutes so that you can crush it.

This recipe comes from the Valencian Rice Farmers' Union. I tasted it at the house of a friend who actually grows rice himself, and immediately asked for it. The true, traditional *paella* made near the Albufera lake only included chicken, eels, snails and large, flat local green beans, but it is made differently everywhere and can include all sorts of meat, sausages, fish, shellfish and vegetables.

For four people use a *paella* with a diameter of about 40 cm (16 cm). If you can't deal with the snails, replace with the rosemary, or with prawns or, if you prefer an entirely meat dish, little pieces of pork.

Serves 4

1 medium chicken, cut into 14 or 16 pieces
salt
100 ml (3½ fl. oz) olive oil
1 medium tomato, skinned, seeded and
chopped
1 clove of garlic, peeled and chopped
350 g (12 oz) green beans (podded broad,
say, or chopped runners)

150 g (5 oz) shelled peas
5 ml (1 tsp) paprika
1.25 litres (2¼ pints) water
3 ml (½ tsp) saffron
12 snails, or a sprig of fresh rosemary
400 g (14 oz) short-grain rice
2 lemons

Season the chicken. Heat the olive oil in the *paella*, and when hot, sauté the pieces of chicken for 5 minutes. Add the tomato, garlic, beans and peas. Stir in the paprika and the water. When the liquid boils add the saffron and snails (or rosemary). Season, lower the heat and simmer for about 20 minutes.

For the rice you'll need a litre or a little more of stock – you can take some out, or reserve a little extra in case you need to add it later. Now turn up the heat, and add the rice to the *paella* as evenly as possible. After about 5 minutes turn down the heat and cook until done – about 12–15 minutes. Shake the pan occasionally. Leave your *paella* to rest for about 5 minutes before serving with wedges of lemon.

COCIDO MADRILEÑO
Boiled Meat and Vegetables
Madrid

This is another of Spain's great dishes which has been made for centuries in one form or another. It evolved from the farmer's *olla podrida* or 'rotten pot' (don't be put off by the name!), which used to boil away by itself, needing practically no attention. It consists of boiled meats, sausages, vegetables and chickpeas, and can be eaten in various ways. The stock – like that of the Italian *bollito misto* – can form the basis of a soup eaten before the meats.

The *Cocido Madrileño* is best eaten on a cold winter's day, but don't expect to go rushing about after lunch as it needs quite some digesting. Restaurants usually serve *cocido* regularly once a week, often on Thursdays, and, depending on where you go, the dish will include more or less ingredients and vary in price as well. *Cocido* soup is often on a menu by itself.

You'll need at least two very large and thick saucepans, plus a frying pan.

COCIDO MADRILEÑO/BOILED MEAT AND VEGETABLES

Serves 4

FORCEMEAT
(can be prepared the day before)
2 eggs
120 g (4½ oz) fresh breadcrumbs
½ clove of garlic, peeled and chopped
5 ml (1 tsp) finely chopped parsley
plain flour
oil for frying

FIRST POT
400 g (14 oz) chickpeas, soaked overnight
in plenty of warm water with a little salt
salt and pepper
400 g (14 oz) topside, top rump or brisket
of beef
½ boiling fowl
1 ham bone
100 g (4 oz) salt belly pork
4 marrow bones
about 3 litres (5¼ pints) water
1 onion, peeled
1 turnip, peeled, whole unless very big
4 medium carrots, scraped
3 medium potatoes, peeled
100 g (4 oz) chorizo sausage

SECOND POT AND FRYING PAN
1 small cabbage, coarsely shredded
150 g (5 oz) morcilla (a black sausage,
rather like black pudding, made with or
without rice)
50 ml (2 fl. oz) olive oil
2 cloves of garlic, peeled and sliced

TO SERVE
fine pasta or rice for the soup
tomato sauce (optional)

To make the forcemeat, beat the eggs, and add the breadcrumbs, garlic and parsley. Season, mix well and shape into balls (the Spanish call them *pelotas*). Dip in flour and fry in oil for a few minutes until golden.

Take the first large thick saucepan and put in

the beef, boiling fowl, ham bone, pork and marrow bones (you can seal the ends of these with a paste of flour and water). Cover with the water and bring to the boil. Skim and add the chickpeas. (In Spain they all go into a special net: this makes it easier to take them out separately.) Lower the heat slightly and boil for approximately 2 hours.

Add the onion, turnip and carrots and cook for another 20 minutes then add the forcemeat, potatoes and *chorizo*. Season, and cook for another 20–30 minutes when the *cocido* should be ready. The time can vary depending on the toughness of the meat and the type of chickpea.

Meanwhile in another saucepan boil the cabbage in water or some stock from the *cocido* with the *morcilla*. When the cabbage is done, about 10 minutes, remove the sausage and slice. Drain the cabbage well. Heat the oil in a frying pan, sauté the

garlic then add the cabbage. Continue to sauté for about 5 minutes, stirring and turning the cabbage over. Keep hot.

Now to make the soup, take sufficient stock from the first saucepan. Bring to the boil in another pan, add pasta or rice to taste, adjust the seasoning and serve when it is done.

The *cocido* is served after the soup on two dishes: one has the chickpeas, vegetables, potatoes and cabbage; another has the meats, fowl and sausages, cut into pieces, plus the marrow bones. Some people like to leave a little soup in their plate and eat the meats in that; others like another, clean, plate, and some tomato sauce with the meat and vegetables.

Spanish housewives do wonders with the leftovers: croquettes are made from the fowl, purée from the chickpeas, or an excellent rice dish.

VERDURAS RELLENAS
Stuffed Vegetables
Madrid

Curiously enough this excellent dish is not easy to find in restaurants in Madrid. It was once on the menu of one called *Mi Pueblo*. The enterprising owner of this restaurant, an American called Dick Stephens, now owns a very smart restaurant called *La Gamella* where one can eat some highly original, Spanish-inspired cooking. *Mi Pueblo* still exists, though, and maybe the dish is still on the menu. In case it isn't, here we go.

Per person

1 tomato
1 onion
1 courgette, cut in 5 cm (2 in) pieces
1 small green pepper
1 potato, scrubbed
olive oil
white wine and water to cook

MEAT STUFFING
the inside of the onion, chopped
2 cloves of garlic, peeled and chopped
100 g (4 oz) meat, finely minced
pine kernels
salt and pepper
1 egg, beaten

Try and have all the vegetables more or less evenly sized. Hollow them out with a teaspoon, removing seeds if necessary. Cut the bottoms straight so they will stand up nicely.

Now prepare the meat stuffing. Sauté the chopped onion and garlic in a little olive oil for a few minutes. Stir in the minced meat. Add a few pine kernels and season. Cook for a minute or two, stirring all the time, then remove from the heat and mix in the egg to bind. Stuff the vegetables with this mixture.

In a large casserole, place first the potatoes, onions and peppers with a little olive oil and white wine around them (about 2.5 cm/1 in depth). Bring to the boil and simmer. After about 15 minutes add the courgettes and finally the tomatoes. Top up if necessary with wine and water and cook, covered, until the vegetables are done, about an hour. The liquid should only come about halfway up the vegetables.

AGRICULTURAL LANDSCAPE OF LA MANCHA, AN AREA WHERE SAFFRON CROCUSES ARE GROWN.

THE RED STIGMA OF SAFFRON IS SEPARATED FROM THE MAUVE CROCUS FLOWERS. (PHOTO BY SANTIAGO MUELAS, ASPECT PICTURE LIBRARY)

PIMIENTOS RELLENOS
Stuffed Peppers
Nationwide

This recipe can be made with fresh red or green peppers or tinned *pimientos*. If you are using fresh ones, first char them under a grill or in the oven to remove the skins (see page 22).

Serves 4

8 medium mixed peppers
salt and pepper

SAUCE
1 onion, peeled and finely chopped
1 carrot, scraped and chopped
45 ml (3 tbsp) olive oil
15 ml (1 tbsp) tomato purée
5 ml (1 tsp) chopped parsley
15 ml (1 tbsp) plain flour
150 ml (5 fl. oz) white wine
100 ml (3½ fl. oz) water

STUFFING
60 ml (4 tbsp) olive oil
1 onion, peeled and finely chopped
1 clove of garlic, peeled and finely chopped
10 ml (2 tsp) chopped parsley
250 g (9 oz) minced meat (any will do, to taste)
65 g (2½ oz) fresh breadcrumbs, soaked in a little milk

For the sauce, gently fry the onion and carrot in the oil. Add the tomato purée, parsley and flour. Stir well and cook for a minute then add the white wine, cold water and some salt and pepper. Bring to the boil, reduce the heat, cover and cook slowly whilst you prepare the stuffing.

Heat the oil in a frying pan then add the onion, garlic and parsley and sauté for a few minutes. Next add the meat. Mix the ingredients well and cook for a few minutes. Add the squeezed dry breadcrumbs, season with some salt and pepper, and cook for another 4 minutes, stirring all the time.

Stuff the peppers with the mixture and put them in an ovenproof dish. Sieve the sauce or purée it in a liquidizer. Pour into the dish and cook in a moderate oven – 190°C (375°F) Gas 5 – for half an hour.

PIMIENTOS RELLENOS/STUFFED PEPPERS

RABO DE BUEY ESTILO JUANA
Braised Oxtail
Malaga

At one of Madrid's most famous restaurants, founded by a German, Otto Horcher, in the forties, I often used to eat oxtail when I went there in the sixties with my father-in-law. He not only knew the owner well, but was a great lover of German specialities. Not long ago when lunching there I made a comment about the delicious oxtail, and found out that now there was nothing German about it as the chef responsible for it came from Malaga.

Serves 4

16 pieces of oxtail
2 onions, peeled and diced
4 carrots, scraped and diced
2 leeks, cleaned and chopped in neat
rounds
2 sticks of celery, scraped and chopped
2 bay leaves
a sprig of thyme
1.5 litres (2½ pints) red wine
100 ml (3½ fl. oz) olive oil
30 ml (2 tbsp) tomato purée
salt and pepper

Marinate the oxtail, vegetables, bay leaves and thyme in the red wine overnight – if you leave it longer, then even better.

Heat the oil in a pan and sauté the oxtail quickly on all sides and then transfer to a heavy casserole. Sauté the vegetables, add the tomato purée and mix into the oxtail. Add the wine you have marinated the oxtail in. Season and simmer for about 2 hours. Adjust seasoning and serve.

Boiled or mashed potatoes go very well with this dish.

HIGADO CON CEBOLLA Y AJO
Liver with Onions and Garlic
Nationwide

This is very good made either with calf's or lamb's liver. In Spain the offal, or *asadura*, from baby lamb is often cooked in this way.

Serves 4

> 500 g (18 oz) liver, cut into square chunks
> salt and pepper
> 45 ml (3 tbsp) finely chopped parsley
> 100 ml (3½ fl. oz) olive oil
> 2 cloves of garlic, peeled and sliced
> 5 ml (1 tsp) paprika
> 200 ml (7 fl. oz) dry white wine
> 400 g (14 oz) onions, peeled and finely diced

(*LEFT*) THE WINE MUSEUM IN THE CELLARS UNDER THE CARMEN DE PERELADA CHURCH, CATALONIA.

(*RIGHT*) A MARKET IN MADRID.

Put the chopped liver in a bowl and sprinkle with the salt, pepper and parsley. Heat the oil in a frying pan and sauté the garlic. When it is golden remove from the pan and crush with the paprika in a little of the wine.

Now sauté the onions in the oil until golden, then increase the heat and quickly sauté the pieces of liver. Add the garlic mixture and the rest of the wine to the pan, and mix all the ingredients together. Cover and sauté for about 5 minutes. Very little liquid should be left.

TERNERA GUISADA CON SETAS
Veal Stewed with Mushrooms
Madrid

This recipe can be made with either beef or veal. It is very good made with *niscalos*, fungi that grow in profusion in the Basque Country in autumn. They are sent to many parts of Spain and in particular to Catalonia, where they are called *rovellon*. These orangey mushrooms – *Lactarius deliciosus*, or saffron milk-cap – are extremely gritty and need washing several times.

Serves 4

750 g (a good 1½ lb) good stewing steak,
cut into chunks
30 g (1¼ oz) plain flour
100 ml (3½ fl. oz) olive oil
1 onion, peeled and diced
250 ml (8 fl. oz) water
250 ml (8 fl. oz) Malaga wine or sweet
sherry
salt and pepper
600 g (1 lb, 5 oz) mushrooms, very well
washed, quartered
30 g (1¼ oz) cornflour (optional)
5 ml (1 tsp) chopped parsley

Dip the meat in the flour. Heat the oil in a casserole and fry the meat chunks until golden on all sides. Remove and sauté the onion until transparent in the remaining oil. (If necessary add a little more oil.) Return the meat to the casserole, cover with the water and wine, season and bring to the boil. Lower the heat and simmer for 30–45 minutes, depending on the toughness of the meat.

After 30 minutes add the mushrooms and a little more liquid if necessary, and cook for another half an hour. Adjust the seasoning and if necessary thicken the sauce slightly. Dissolve the cornflour in a little water, add to the sauce, and bring to the boil, stirring all the time. Cook for a minute or two and then serve in the casserole, garnished with chopped parsley.

SOUTHERN VINEYARDS OF THE RIOJA REGION.

TERNERA GUISADA CON SETAS/VEAL STEWED WITH MUSHROOMS

116

RIÑONES AL JEREZ
Kidneys in Sherry
Nationwide

Veal kidneys are easy to find in Spain. More often than not the butcher brings them out of the refrigerator, removes the outer fat, and then chops them into the small pieces required for this dish.

Never overcook kidneys as they will become hard. Also it is essential to soak them for at least an hour in cold water to which you have added a little lemon juice. Change the water once or twice, or put them under the running tap for a few minutes, then they ought not to taste unpleasant. The darker the kidneys the older the animal they come from and therefore they'll probably need more soaking than the paler ones. By the way this dish is equally good made with lamb's or chicken livers.

Serves 4

750 g (a good 1½ lb) veal (or lamb's)
kidneys, trimmed and cored
100 ml (3½ fl. oz) olive oil
1 medium onion, peeled and diced
350 ml (12 fl. oz) dry sherry
150 ml (5 fl. oz) water
salt and pepper
cornflour if necessary

Cut the kidneys into small pieces, removing any gristle or fat.

Heat the olive oil in a pan or casserole and sauté the onion until it starts to become transparent. Add the kidneys and stir for about 5 minutes over a medium heat. Next add 250 ml (8 fl. oz) of the sherry and the water, season and turn up the heat. When it

boils, immediately lower the heat and simmer for about 15 minutes with the lid on. Adjust the seasoning and add the rest of the sherry.

If you would like the sauce a little thicker, dissolve a little cornflour in a little water and stir in gently until it has reached the right consistency. Otherwise cook for a minute more and serve.

I think this dish improves if made in advance and reheated, which is when you add the remainder of the sherry. Plain boiled rice goes very well with the kidneys. Any that are left over are delicious baked with an egg in a ramekin as a first course.

CERDO CON SALSA DE NUECES
Pork in Walnut Sauce
Galicia

Galicia in north-western Spain is famous for its *lacon*, a variety of boiled ham, which is excellent eaten either hot or cold. This pork recipe also comes from Galicia, although I have eaten it in Madrid in private houses.

Serves 6

1.5 kg (3½ lb) lean pork (any joint will do)
coarse salt and freshly ground black pepper
15 g (½ oz) butter
freshly grated nutmeg
15 ml (1 tbsp) brandy (optional)
1 litre (1¾ pints) milk
150 g (5 oz) shelled walnuts, scalded and
peeled

Sprinkle the pork with salt and leave for about an hour. Preheat the oven to 200°C (400°F) Gas 6.

Rub the meat with the butter, and season it with nutmeg and pepper. Brown in a pan on all sides, then flame with the brandy. Place the meat on a low rack (or upturned plate) in a fairly deep dish that will hold the meat snugly, cover with milk and cook in the oven for about 1½ hours. (You can also cook it on top of the stove over a low flame if you prefer.) After about half an hour add the walnuts, which I have to admit I hardly ever scald and peel! Adjust the seasoning. You can add more milk if necessary.

When the meat is cooked, remove it, slice it, and serve the sauce separately. Mashed potato is the best accompaniment. Baked apple slices also go well. Just slice the apples and bake them with a little butter, salt, a few drops of lemon juice and a pinch of cinnamon.

CHORIZO SAUSAGES, A SPECIALITY OF NAVARRA, HANGING ON DISPLAY.

CHULETAS DE CERDO CON JAMÓN Y VINO BLANCO
Pork Chops with Ham and White Wine
Aragon

Pork is eaten widely in Spain and in fact almost every part of the animal is made use of, from the trotters to the ears!

Serves 4–5

1 kg (2¼ lb) pork chops, cut fairly thin
50 g (2 oz) flour
100 g (4 oz) lard or 100 ml (3½ fl. oz) olive oil
200 g (7 oz) ham, diced
1 medium onion, peeled and diced
3 medium tomatoes, skinned, seeded and chopped
250 ml (8 fl. oz) white wine
1 hard-boiled egg, chopped
salt and pepper

Dip the chops in flour on both sides. Heat the lard or oil in a casserole and fry them quickly on both sides. Remove the chops and then sauté the ham and onion in the remaining fat. When the onion starts to become transparent add the tomato and sauté for 2–3 minutes, stirring all the time. Next add the white wine and cook for another minute or two.

Return the chops to the casserole and sprinkle in the chopped egg. Season and cover, then simmer until the chops are done – about 45 minutes. (You can also bake them in the oven.) Mashed potato goes nicely with this dish.

CHULETAS DE CERDO CON ALCAPARRAS
Pork Chops with Capers
Andalusia

The piquant flavour of the capers and gherkins complements the richness of the pork nicely.

Serves 4

750 g (a good 1½ lb) pork chops, cut fairly
thin
salt and pepper
25 g (1 oz) plain flour
50 g (2 oz) lard
250 ml (8 fl. oz) meat stock
15 ml (1 tbsp) white wine vinegar
25 g (1 oz) capers, chopped
25 g (1 oz) gherkins, chopped

Cut any surplus fat off the chops, season them and dip in flour on both sides. Heat the lard in a saucepan or casserole, and sauté the chops, turning frequently until they are golden on both sides.

Add the stock and vinegar to the casserole, bring to the boil and cover. Turn down the heat and simmer for 15 minutes. Before serving add the capers and gherkins.

CALDERETA DE CORDERO
Lamb Stew
Extremadura

One of Extremadura's best dishes, this *caldereta* – which refers to the iron cooking pot – can be made from either baby lamb or kid. If you make it with older meat then stew for longer.

Pimiento morrón is a tinned peeled red pepper. If you use dried peppers instead, seed and chop and add with the onion.

Serves 6

1.5 kg (3½ lb) lamb, cut in small pieces
salt
100 ml (3½ fl. oz) olive oil
3 cloves of garlic, peeled
200 g (7 oz) lamb's liver in one piece
200 g (7 oz) onions, peeled and chopped
1 large bay leaf
5 ml (1 tsp) paprika
500 ml (18 fl. oz) dry white wine
10 ml (2 tsp) plain flour
500 ml (18 fl. oz) meat stock
6 black peppercorns
1 pimiento morrón, or dried sweet pepper
(see above)
15 ml (1 tbsp) chopped parsley

Season the lamb with salt. Heat the oil in a casserole (reserve 5 ml/1 tsp). Gently fry the whole cloves of garlic, and when golden, remove put to one side. Next add the pieces of lamb and the piece of liver to the casserole. Turn the meat over a hot flame until done on all sides. Remove the liver and keep to one side. Next add the onion and bay leaf, sauté well and sprinkle with the paprika. Add the wine and continue to turn the pieces of lamb whilst the wine reduces. Sprinkle in the flour and stir in well. Next add the stock or water, cover and stew for about 45 minutes. Meanwhile crush together the peppercorns, the fried garlic, the *pimiento morrón* and the

reserved oil. Crush the liver with these ingredients or give it a whirl in a liquidizer with some of the liquid from the stew. Add this paste to the lamb which should be tender by now. Sprinkle with chopped parsley. Cook for another 10 minutes.

CORDERO A LA ALMENDRA
Lamb with Flaked Almonds
Levante

This recipe comes from an excellent restaurant in Murcia in the east of Spain, called *El Rincon de Pepe*, where you can eat the most wonderful fish baked in salt among other things.

Serves 4

250 g (9 oz) lard
4 cloves of garlic, peeled and cut into slivers
1 large onion, peeled and cut into strips
1 leg of lamb weighing about 1.5 kg (3 lb, 5 oz), chopped into thick slices (boned if like)
50 g (2 oz) flour
1 large, ripe tomato, skinned, seeded and chopped
200 ml (7 fl. oz) white wine
100 ml (3½ fl. oz) brandy
1 litre (1¾ pints) water
100 g (4 oz) almonds, blanched and slivered
12 strands of saffron
5 ml (1 tsp) chopped parsley
3 ml (½ tsp) dried thyme
salt and pepper

Melt the lard in a thick casserole. Add the sliced garlic and the onion. Sauté for 2–3 minutes until the onion is transparent. Dip the pieces of lamb in the flour and then sauté in the pan with the onions and garlic for about 10 minutes. Next add the tomato and cook for 4–5 minutes. Add the wine and brandy, cook for a minute and then add the water. Bring to the boil and add most of the almonds, the saffron, parsley and thyme. Season with pepper and salt and cook slowly, covered, until the meat is tender – about 45 minutes – depending on the lamb.

Just before serving, add the rest of the almonds. If you like you can pour off the sauce, process it then cover the lamb with it and garnish with the slivered almonds.

VINEYARDS STRETCHING ACROSS THE LANDSCAPE OF PRIORATO, IN THE RUGGED MOUNTAIN COUNTRY OF CATALONIA.

CORDERO ASADO
Roast Lamb
Castile

If you can get baby lamb then roast it as it is done in Spain with very little fat and some water. The meat is so good it needs little embellishing. Baby lambs are slaughtered from a month to three months. From the name *cordero lechal* (*lechal* derives from milk), we can deduce they have only been fed on milk. The *Cordero Pascual* which abounds in the spring, and at *Pascua* or Easter, can be up to a year old, and is also delicious.

About 30 minutes per kg (2¼ lb) is the average roasting time, but a lot depends on how large a piece of meat you have, and how well cooked you like it.

Serves 6

> *a ½ lamb, approx. 2–3 kg (4½–7 lb)*
> *salt and pepper*

> *VERSION 1*
> *2 cloves of garlic, peeled and halved*
> *50 g (2 oz) lard*
> *400 ml (14 fl. oz) water*
> *150 ml (5 fl. oz) brandy (optional)*

> *VERSION 2*
> *25 g (1 oz) lard or 25 ml (1 fl. oz) olive oil*
> *2 cloves of garlic, peeled*
> *25 ml (1 fl. oz) wine vinegar*
> *100 ml (3½ fl. oz) white wine*

Cut the lamb into quarters, and sprinkle with salt. Preheat the oven to 200°C (400°F) Gas 6.

For the first version, rub the pieces of lamb with

RICE FIELD IN SPAIN. (PHOTO BY C.D. GEISSLER, THE IMAGE BANK)

garlic and half the lard. Put the lamb in an earthenware dish with the water, and roast for about 20 minutes. Turn the pieces, and add the rest of the lard. Continue roasting at 180°C (350°F) Gas 4, and add more hot water if necessary (or the brandy which gives it a nice golden colour). Baste frequently during the remainder of the cooking time (see introduction).

For the second version, rub the lamb with a little oil or lard. Put it into the same hot oven until it starts to turn golden. Meanwhile boil the whole cloves of garlic in the vinegar and white wine mixture, then remove the garlic. Baste the lamb with this for the remainder of the cooking time (at the lower temperature).

Yet another version uses lemon juice and rosemary or thyme to baste the meat. It's hard to say which is the best . . .

ALBÓNDIGAS
Meat Balls
Nationwide

This recipe is actually typical of La Mancha, but similar versions are eaten all over Spain. You could use Valdepeñas white wine for this recipe, or I sometimes use sherry. Diced, boiled potatoes or plain boiled rice go very well with this dish.

Serves 4

400 g (14 oz) boned leg of lamb, minced
100 g (4 oz) lean pork, minced
3 cloves of garlic, peeled and finely chopped
100 g (4 oz) fresh breadcrumbs, soaked in a little water

1 hard-boiled egg, chopped
salt and pepper
50 g (2 oz) plain flour
vegetable oil for frying
25 g (1 oz) lard
3 ml (½ tsp) paprika
250 ml (8 fl. oz) white wine
250 ml (8 fl. oz) meat stock
30 ml (2 tbsp) tomato purée
5 ml (1 tsp) chopped parsley

Mix the meats, two-thirds of the chopped garlic, the breadcrumbs (which you have squeezed out), the hard-boiled egg and seasoning. Work together with your hands and form into rounds the size of a walnut. Roll in half the flour. Heat enough oil in a frying pan and shallow-fry the meatballs quickly on all sides until they are golden. (You'll need to do this in batches.) Drain and place in a casserole, cover and keep hot.

In another pan heat the lard and sauté the remaining chopped garlic. Stir in the rest of the flour and cook for a minute or two, stirring all the time over a gentle heat, then add the paprika, white wine and stock. Bring gently to the boil, add the tomato purée and adjust the seasoning. Simmer for about 10 minutes, covered, then put through a mouli or work in a processor.

Pour the sauce over the *albóndigas* in the casserole, and cook gently for about 20 minutes. Before serving sprinkle with the chopped parsley.

POLLO CHILINDRÓN
Chicken with Red Peppers
Aragon

Chilindrón is a sauce typical of Aragon in east-central Spain, which includes red peppers. If you are driving through Spain it is quite likely you'll pass through Saragossa, the *chilindrón* capital where, at any of the little restaurants in the district known as El Tubo, you'll be able to try not only chicken, but lamb and maybe rabbit or pork done in this way. The dark, heavy-bodied Aragonese wine makes a perfect accompaniment to this slightly piquant dish.

Serves 4

> *2 large or 4 medium red peppers*
> *1 medium chicken, cut into joints*
> *salt and pepper*
> *200 ml (7 fl. oz) olive oil*
> *1 clove of garlic, peeled and sliced*
> *1 onion, peeled and diced*
> *1 chilli pepper, cut into rings (optional)*
> *200 g (7 oz) cured ham, diced*
> *1 kg (2¼ lb) tomatoes, skinned, seeded and chopped*

Char the peppers (see page 22), then peel and seed them. Cut them into medium-sized pieces. Season the pieces of chicken.

Heat the oil in a casserole and fry the garlic. Next add the chicken and brown on all sides. Add the onion, the chilli if you are using it, and the ham. Sauté for a few minutes and when the onion starts to turn golden add the pepper pieces. Stir well and add the tomatoes.

Cover and cook slowly until the chicken is done and the sauce has evaporated – about 30–45 minutes. There should be very little liquid left. You can always remove the lid if it needs reducing.

THE WINE MUSEUM OF *BODEGAS ASCENCIO CARCELÉN* IN JUMILLA IN THE LEVANTE REGION.

POLLO CHILINDRÓN/CHICKEN WITH RED PEPPERS

POLLO AL AJILLO
Chicken Fried in Garlic
Nationwide

A very popular dish, which is quick and easy to prepare. It is excellent eaten cold (very suitable for picnics), and reheats well. It is a matter of taste whether you eat it dry and crispy or in its garlic sauce. I usually start by eating the chicken and then dip pieces of bread into the sauce, then can't resist the temptation to eat the fried pieces of garlic. The sauce is also good if you add a dash of sherry to it just before serving. Do it *off* the heat, says the voice of experience, or you may well set the house on fire!

Serves 4

a medium chicken cut into pieces
salt and pepper
100 ml (3½ fl. oz) olive oil
8–10 cloves of garlic, peeled and thickly
sliced
a dash of sherry or brandy (optional)

Wipe and dry the pieces of chicken, and season with salt and pepper. Heat the oil in a thick frying pan, and brown the chicken on all sides. Add the garlic, lower the flame slightly and cover with a lid. Cook until done – about 15 minutes – turning occasionally. Turn up the heat and add the sherry if you wish. Either remove the pieces of chicken and serve, or leave them for longer in the sauce, in which case they won't be as crispy, but are also good.

If you like hot dishes, another idea is to add a couple of pieces of chilli pepper to the garlic.

POLLO EN SANFAINA
Chicken with Aubergines
Catalonia

Sanfaina is one of the four main Catalan 'sauces', and it includes aubergines, courgettes, onions, peppers and tomatoes. Each cook varies the amounts to his or her own taste.

Serves 4

1 large chicken, jointed
salt and pepper
300 g (11 oz) red or green peppers, or both
300 g (11 oz) aubergines, peeled and sliced
fairly thickly
300 g (11 oz) courgettes, peeled and sliced
fairly thickly
200 ml (7 fl. oz) olive oil
500 g (18 oz) onions, peeled and cut into
strips
200 g (7 oz) cured ham, diced
1 clove of garlic, peeled and finely chopped
750 g (a good 1½ lb) tomatoes, skinned,
seeded and chopped
150 ml (5 fl. oz) white wine
1 bay leaf

Season the chicken with salt and pepper. Char the peppers (see page 22), then peel, seed and dice. Sprinkle the aubergine and courgette slices with salt and leave for about half an hour. Wash and dry well.

Heat just over half the oil in a fireproof dish or casserole and sauté the chicken pieces until golden. Next add the onions, pepper dice, ham and garlic. Stir and cook until the onion begins to turn golden. Add the tomatoes and allow to fry for about 5 min-

utes. Add the wine and bay leaf and cover the cas-serole and simmer gently while you cook the vegetables. (You can always add a little stock or water.)

Meanwhile heat the rest of the oil in another pan, and sauté the aubergine and courgette slices until golden. Season and add to the casserole. Con-tinue simmering gently until the chicken is cooked – about another 30–45 minutes. The liquid should evaporate, as the sauce ought to be thick. Remove the bay leaf. Serve the chicken on a dish, and spoon the sauce over.

GALLINA EN PEPITORIA
Boiling Fowl Stewed with Almonds
Madrid

This recipe can be made with chicken but it tastes much better with boiling fowl, although of course it takes longer to cook and the flavour is quite dif-ferent. Similar dishes are eaten in many parts of Spain. In the Rioja walnuts are added instead of al-monds, and in Andalusia egg yolk is used to thicken the sauce which is also very good.

If you are in Madrid, try it at *Ciriaco*.

Serves 4–6

1 large boiling fowl
plain flour for coating
75 ml (5 tbsp) olive oil
1 medium onion, peeled and finely chopped
1 clove of garlic, peeled
1 bay leaf
30 ml (2 tbsp) pine kernels

a few strands of saffron
15 almonds
15 ml (1 tbsp) chopped parsley
salt and pepper
100 ml (3½ fl. oz) dry white wine
2 hard-boiled eggs

Joint the bird into six pieces, and dip these in flour. Heat the oil in a frying pan, and fry the chicken on all all sides. When golden, put on a plate. Gently sauté the finely chopped onion, whole clove of garlic and bay leaf: after a minute or two add the pine kernels and stir. Remove the contents of the pan and crush slightly with the saffron, almonds, parsley and some salt, either in a pestle and mortar, or with a quick whirl in a liquidizer.

Now place the pieces of boiling fowl in a cas-serole and add the white wine and contents of the mortar. Cover with water and cook slowly for about 2 hours. It depends upon how tough the fowl is.

Just before serving mash the egg yolks with a fork in a little of the stock from the casserole. Chop the whites and add both yolk and white to the stew. Adjust seasoning, and serve either in the casserole or in a dish. You can garnish it with triangles of fried bread. Plain boiled rice goes well too.

(*OVERLEAF*) NAVARRA LANDSCAPE.

PAVO A LA CATALANA
Turkey Stuffed with Dried Fruit and Nuts
Catalonia

Turkey has never been traditional Christmas fare in Spain except in Catalonia and Andalusia. Nowadays, however, it is eaten more and more all over the country, mainly on Christmas Eve, which is when the main celebrations are. At one of my favourite restaurants in Barcelona, *Can Culleretes*, which is over 200 years old, you can eat turkey nearly all year round.

Serves 6–8
> *1 turkey, preferably a hen, approx. 4–5 kg*
> *(9–11 lb)*
> *salt and pepper*
> *butter and dripping for roasting*

> *STUFFING*
> *250 g (9 oz) sausagemeat*
> *25 g (1 oz) chopped onion*
> *100 g (4 oz) raisins*
> *150 g (5 oz) prunes, stoned and chopped*
> *150 g (5 oz) dates, stoned and chopped*
> *150 g (5 oz) dried apricots or peaches, chopped*
> *150 g (5 oz) dried figs, chopped*
> *50 g (2 oz) almonds*
> *50 g (2 oz) pine kernels*
> *100 ml (3½ fl. oz) brandy or port*

Make the stuffing first. Fry the sausagemeat gently in a little butter with the onion, and then add the dried fruit, nuts, pine kernels, seasoning and brandy or port. Mix well then stuff the turkey.

Preheat the oven to 220°C (425°F) Gas 7. Season the bird well, then cover the breast generously with butter so that it doesn't get dry. Cover the breast with foil. Roast for 30 minutes then turn the oven down to 170°C (325°F) Gas 3. Roast for a further 3–3½ hours, basting occasionally. Re-cover with the foil each time. Remove foil about half an hour before the end of this time and turn the oven up again, to 200°C (400°F) Gas 6 so that the breast browns nicely. Baste frequently during this time. Test to see that the bird is cooked by piercing the thickest part of the leg with a skewer; if pink juices run out the turkey must be cooked for a little longer.

Carve the turkey and serve surrounded with the stuffing.

You can also make this dish with a capon or large chicken; adjust the proportion of stuffing and the cooking times accordingly.

PAVO EN PEPITORIA
Turkey Stewed in Saffron
Andalusia

Although not common in the old days in other parts of Spain except for Catalonia, turkey has always been eaten in most parts of Andalusia. Turkey is now found in markets, at least in Madrid, all the year round.

Serves 6
> *1 young turkey, about 3 kg (7 lb), jointed*
> *200 g (7 oz) lard*
> *2 cloves of garlic, peeled and sliced*
> *2 slices of bread*

20 g (¾ oz) parsley leaves
1 medium onion, peeled and finely chopped
2 cloves
10 ml (2 tsp) saffron
1 small bay leaf
25 g (1 oz) cornflour (optional)

Wipe and dry the turkey pieces.

Melt half the lard in a large casserole and sauté the garlic and bread until golden. Remove and add the rest of the lard to the pan. Heat, then pop the parsley in for a few seconds and remove. Next sauté the onion until transparent, about 2–3 minutes, and then add the pieces of turkey. Sauté on all sides until golden, then cover with water, bring to the boil, cover and simmer for about 45 minutes.

Meanwhile crush the garlic and bread with the cloves, saffron and the bay leaf which you have toasted briefly in a flame. Make this into a paste with a little of the turkey stock and add to the casserole. Mix in well and continue to simmer until the turkey is tender, about another 30 minutes. You can always add more water if necessary.

When the turkey is done, put on a serving dish and keep warm. If you want to thicken the sauce, dissolve the cornflour in a little cold water and stir into the turkey stock. Bring slowly to the boil, stirring all the time. Lower the heat and cook for a minute and then pour over the turkey and serve.

CORDORNICES ASADAS CON HOJAS DE VID
Roast Quails in Vine Leaves
Andalusia

As quails are now farmed they are easy to find. This is an excellent way of cooking them, as the vine leaves ensure that they remain moist and tender.

Serves 4

8 quails
salt and pepper
100 ml (3½ fl. oz) brandy (optional)
8 vine leaves
8 thick slices of bacon
juice of 1 lemon

Preheat the oven to 200°C (400°F) Gas 6. Season the inside of the quails with salt and pepper. If you are using brandy, spoon a little into each one. Wrap each bird in a piece of bacon, then a vine leaf and secure with a piece of thread. Roast in the oven with no extra fat for about 15 minutes.

Put on a serving dish and keep warm. Add the lemon juice to the juices in the roasting tin, heat briefly then pour over the quails and serve.

PERDICES CON CHOCOLATE
Partridges in Chocolate Sauce
Castile

The partridge shooting season starts in Spain on the second Sunday in October. The Spanish partridge, which is the red variety, is shot in many parts of Spain, but the best are found on the plains of La Mancha. There are many ways of cooking part-ridges, from roasting to casseroling them in all sorts of sauces. Naturally what you do with them very much depends on whether they are young or old birds, or if you have actually been given them and been able to hang them. Game is practically never hung in Spain and the insides are removed very quickly, so if you buy a bird in a market, I'd nearly always casserole it as it is most likely to be pretty tough.

This is rather an unusual recipe, but the choco-late gives the sauce a lovely consistency.

Serves 4

4 partridges (you can serve ½ per person)
salt and pepper
12 chestnuts
60 ml (4 tbsp) olive oil
3 cloves of garlic, peeled and chopped
15 ml (1 tbsp) wine vinegar
500 ml (18 fl. oz) meat or chicken stock
100 ml (3½ fl. oz) white wine
2 medium onions, peeled and chopped
2 pears, peeled and halved
90 g (3½ oz) chocolate (the unsweetened
plain dark sort), grated
4 rounds of fried bread
a handful of raisins
chopped parsley

Season the partridges with salt and pepper, and put the chestnuts in boiling water so you'll be able to peel them more easily.

Heat the oil, add the chopped garlic and brown the birds on all sides. Then add the vinegar, stock, wine and onion, bring to the boil, lower the heat, cover and cook gently until tender. If necessary you can add more stock and wine. Depending on how tough the birds are, cooking can take from 1–2 hours.

In a separate saucepan cook the peeled chestnuts in a little extra stock. When they are nearly ready – after about 20 minutes – add the peeled halved pears. Remove the partridges from the casserole, portion and put in a nice dish with the barely cooked pears and the chestnuts around. Keep warm.

Sieve the sauce you cooked the partridges in. Return to the stove, and add the grated chocolate. Stir for a few minutes until it is a nice consistency, then pour over the partridges and serve hot, gar-nished with rounds or triangles of fried bread, rai-sins and the chopped parsley. Mashed potatoes go well with this dish too.

PERDICES CON CHOCOLATE/PARTRIDGES IN
CHOCOLATE SAUCE

LIEBRE CON JUDIAS
Hare with White Beans
Castile

You can make this recipe with rabbit if you don't like hare, but if you do, then this is an excellent way of eating white beans as it gives them great flavour. I usually make it with the larger type of beans.

Serves 4–6

500 g (18 oz) white beans
1 hare, jointed
150 ml (5 fl. oz) white wine
15 ml (1 tbsp) wine vinegar
1 bay leaf
about 5 black peppercorns
100 ml (3½ fl. oz) olive oil
1 large onion, peeled and diced
2 medium tomatoes, skinned, seeded and
chopped
1 litre (1¾ pints) cold water
2 cloves of garlic, skin on and roasted in the
flame before adding
salt
10 ml (2 tsp) chopped fresh parsley

Soak the beans in cold water overnight, or for at least 3 hours before using. Put the hare in a bowl and pour over a mixture of the wine, vinegar, bay leaf and peppercorns. Allow to stand for at least an hour, turning the pieces. You could do this the night before if you wish, and leave overnight.

Drain the beans, cover with fresh cold water and bring slowly to the boil. Throw away the water and keep beans to one side. This operation is to ensure the beans will not be too hard.

Meanwhile, drain the hare and dry it, keeping any liquid in the bowl. Heat the oil in a fairly large casserole and sauté the pieces of hare on all sides. Remove from the pan and keep warm. Next sauté the onion until transparent then add the tomatoes and sauté for about 5 minutes more. Return the hare to the pan with the strained liquid from the bowl. Mix all together and add the beans. Cover with the measured cold water, add the garlic, bring to the boil, and cook gently until done, about 1–1½ hours.

Season with salt to taste, and serve, after removing the bay leaf and garlic, in the same casserole, sprinkled with parsley. The final dish should not have too much liquid, but enough to use a spoon.

CONEJO CON PERAS
Rabbit with Pears
Catalonia

This excellent recipe was given to me by José María, the owner of the Hotel Boix; this is near the village of Martinet in the Province of Lerida, not far from Andorra. If you are anywhere near I suggest you stop for a meal. In 1987 the readers of one of Spain's best food guides voted it the restaurant of the year, and I have never been disappointed there. Apart from the recipe, I was given home-made jams, herbs from the Cerdanya district, and thyme vinegar.

Serves 4–5

1 kg (2¼ lb) rabbit
salt and pepper
200 g (7 oz) onions, peeled
200 g (7 oz) carrots, scraped
50 g (2 oz) leeks, cleaned
25 g (1 oz) celery, washed

650 g (1 lb, 7 oz) pears (about 6)
250 ml (8 fl. oz) olive oil
100 ml (3½ fl. oz) dry white wine
1 litre (1¾ pints) meat stock
1 clove of garlic, peeled and chopped
15 ml (1 tbsp) chopped parsley
10 almonds and hazelnuts, chopped

Cut the rabbit into twelve pieces. Season with salt and lots of freshly ground black pepper. Clean and roughly chop all the vegetables. Peel and chop two of the pears.

In a casserole heat the olive oil and sauté the rabbit on all sides for about 10 minutes. Remove the casserole from the stove, take out the rabbit and keep warm. Now add the onions, carrots, leeks, celery, chopped pears and wine to the oil in the casserole. Cover with the stock, add the garlic, parsley and nuts, season and boil for 15 minutes. Blend the sauce in a mixer.

Cover the rabbit with the sauce. Test seasoning and cook for 15 minutes, turning the rabbit continuously. Add the four remaining pears, peeled, cored and cut in half. Cook for about 3 minutes.

Put the rabbit pieces in a serving dish, and pour over the sauce. Slice and arrange the pears around.

I have made this recipe with chicken, which is also good.

POSTRES · DESSERTS

When I first came to Spain I was most disappointed by the lack of puddings in ordinary *tascas* or bars. The menu, which was recited off at top speed, always included *'flan, helado y melocotón en almíbar'* – caramel custard, ice cream (usually vanilla) and tinned peaches. At best the speciality might be *suflé Alaska*, a very sweet concoction of vanilla ice cream baked in meringue. However, there were places such as *El Majuelo* where the caramel custard had an orange flavour to it which made it that bit different and delicious. There were other restaurants I discovered later on, such as *Lucio*, where the *natillas* sprinkled with cinnamon bore no resemblance to any custard I'd ever eaten before. Then in Catalonia, *crema Catalana* became one of my favourite puddings together with other Catalan specialities: *musico*, simply a combination of nuts and raisins, *mel i mato*, made from fresh cream cheese and honey, not forgetting those delicious little cakes made with pine kernels called *piñonets*. Along the Cantabrian coast, where there are many diary farms, there are some excellent milk-based puddings such as the *quesada* and rice pudding I have included in the recipes, and light sponge cakes called *sobaos*. Galicia is famous for a sort of pancake called *filloas*, which can either be savoury or sweet, and *tarta de Santiago*, another of my favourite Spanish puddings, which is a pastry case with an almond filling.

Along the east coast it is almonds and honey sweets of Arab origin that head the field, and in the south of Spain again, there are hundreds of little almond, cinnamon and honey goodies that are a sort of cross between a cake and a biscuit, as well as lots of kinds of fritters and *buñuelos*, fried dough-based sweets filled with cream. Anise liqueurs are used to flavour many of those *rosquillas, tortas* or *polvorones*.

Then there are the sweets which are associated with the convents, most of which are made from egg yolks. Some are named after the Virgin and Saints, others simply have wonderful names such as 'nun's sighs' or 'angel's hair', the latter a frequent filling for pastries, made from candied marrow.

Each season seems to have a speciality whether it be *torrijas*, the marzipan 'saint's bones' at Easter (another great favourite), the bun-like *roscon de Reyes* eaten at Epiphany, or my favourite Madrid summer speciality (which is getting harder and harder to find), *leche merengada*, a creamy milk ice cream with cinnamon sprinkled on top.

LA MANCHA'S HERO, DON QUIXOTE, DEPICTED IN A TILE PAINTING OUTSIDE THE TRADITIONAL INN OF *VENTA DEL QUIXOTE* IN PUERTO LÁPICE.

La del alba seria cuarndo
Don Quijote salio de la a venta,
tan contento, tan gallardo, tan
alborozado por verse ya ar~
mado caballero que el gozo
le reventaba por las cinchas
del caballo.

Nivehica. Talavera:

(Don Quijote de la Mancha, cap IV)

CREMA CATALANA
Catalan Custard
Catalonia

This delicious custard is hardly eaten anywhere else in Spain except obviously in Catalan restaurants in other big cities. One large firm has, however, made a very successful iced version.

Serves 4

1 litre (1¾ pints) milk
peel of 1 lemon
2 cinnamon sticks
1 vanilla pod
40 g (1½ oz) arrowroot or 15 ml (1 tbsp)
cornflour
6 egg yolks
200 g (7 oz) sugar

TOPPING
90 g (3½ oz) sugar

Bring the milk slowly to the boil with the lemon peel, cinnamon sticks and vanilla pod. Strain and allow to cool. When it is cool dissolve the arrowroot or cornflour in 30 ml (2 tbsp) of it then mix into the bulk of the milk. Beat the egg yolks with the sugar and mix with the milk and arrowroot. Cook over a moderate heat until it is thick and smooth. Always stir with a wooden spoon in the same direction, for example clockwise. If the milk starts to boil remove from the flame and give it a vigorous stir to release the steam. When it has thickened pour into individual clay or ovenproof dishes.

Allow to cool. Now you can sprinkle the top of each dish with the topping sugar and then caramelise with a hot, metal salamander. If your custard comes straight out of the fridge, you can sprinkle it with sugar and pop it under a hot grill, then serve immediately.

Another method is to dissolve the topping sugar very gently, stirring constantly with a wooden spoon (otherwise it will burn), and pour a little of this caramel over each dish.

CREMA CATALANA/CATALAN CUSTARD

A SELECTION OF DEEP-FRIED BATTER AND PASTRY SWEETS, TOGETHER WITH SPHERICAL *YEMAS* MADE FROM EGG YOLK AND SUGAR

TOCINO DE CIELO
Rich Egg Custard
Andalusia

This sweet, which is very, very sweet, is literally called 'fat from heaven'. I am not quite sure about the origins of the name but it definitely has relevance! All of these sweets including lots of egg yolks were made at convents by the nuns who had been given the surplus yolks by wine-makers; they used the whites only for the clarifying process.

The custards are made in dariole moulds, and some people coat these first with caramel; other, more *'nouvelle'*, cooks pour a raspberry *coulis* over the *tocinos*. I prefer to eat them just as they are, as added caramel makes them even sweeter, and raspberry detracts from their flavour.

Serves 4

350 g (12 oz) sugar
250 ml (8 fl. oz) water
12 egg yolks
5 ml (1 tsp) vanilla essence

Bring the sugar and water to the boil in a large, heavy-based pan, stirring with a wooden spoon, so that the sugar is completely dissolved by the time the water boils. Continue to cook until the syrup falls from the spoon in threads – it will take about 20 minutes. Remove from the heat and allow to cool slightly.

Next beat the egg yolks well and gradually add the syrup except for about 15 ml (1 tbsp) which you keep. Beat in the vanilla.

Pour a little of the reserved syrup into each mould then pour in the creamy custard mixture.

Cover loosely, and cook in water in a bain-marie until set – about 15 minutes. You can test with a knife – if it comes out clean then they are ready. Don't overcook. When the *tocinos* are done, allow them to cool completely before unmoulding.

TOCINO DE CIELO/RICH EGG CUSTARD

139

HELADO DE TURRÓN
Almond Ice Cream
Levante

Spanish *turrón* or nougat is now exported to many parts of the world. The two classical ones are the hard and soft, both of which are made basically from roasted almonds, honey and egg white. Jijona in the Province of Alicante on Spain's east coast is renowned for its *turrónes* which undoubtedly originated from the Arab occupation of Spain.

Turrón is eaten mainly at Christmas time, but ice cream made from *turrón* is good all year round.

Serves 4

500 ml (18 fl. oz) milk
1 cinnamon stick
peel of 1 lemon
3 egg yolks
150 g (5 oz) sugar
200 g (7 oz) soft almond turrón, *very finely chopped*

Bring the milk slowly to the boil in a saucepan with the cinnamon stick and the lemon peel. Beat the egg yolks in a bowl with the sugar. Remove the cinnamon stick and peel from the saucepan and add the milk to the egg and sugar mixture gradually, stirring well with a wooden spoon.

Cook in a bain-marie until the custard thickens. Add the *turrón*, mix in well, and leave to get cold. Freeze for about 2 hours.

QUESADA
Cheesecake
Santander

This is really a 'cheesecake', and it's typical of Cantabria. All the old recipes are made with cream cheese, but I find this one – given to me by my friend Maria Garnica, who runs the Ajedrea Cookery School in Santander – very good and easy to make.

Serves 4

500 ml (18 fl. oz) milk
1 cinnamon stick
peel of 1 lemon
butter
300 g (11 oz) sugar
150 g (5 oz) flour, sieved with a pinch of salt
150 g (5 oz) natural yoghurt
2 eggs
powdered cinnamon

Heat the milk with the cinnamon stick and lemon peel. When it boils remove from heat and keep.

Heat the oven to 180°C (350°F) Gas 4. Grease an appropriately sized tin or tin foil mould generously with butter and put it in the oven. The sides should be about 5 cm (2 in) high as the *quesada* rises slightly.

Beat the sugar and flour with the yoghurt and eggs in a bowl. Beat in the strained milk little by little. Pour the mixture into the hot mould, sprinkle with powdered cinnamon and bake for 45 minutes.

ARROZ CON LECHE
Rice Pudding
Asturias

Rice pudding, although some people's nightmare, can be quite delicious if it is really creamy. It is eaten in many parts of Spain but more in the north where you find the best milk and therefore the best dairy produce. However, nobody makes it like Charo who lives down the road from me and who gave me this recipe. I always do it as she says, but why the milk has to be brought to the boil the night before in *separate* saucepans is still a mystery to me. No doubt someone will enlighten me, but meanwhile I continue to follow on this tradition of her village. The main secret, I think, lies in the fact that Charo's recipe requires twice as much milk as most of the others I've ever seen.

Serves 6

5 litres (8¾ pints) milk
120 g (4½ oz) butter
500 g (18 oz) Spanish short-grain rice
5 ml (1 tsp) salt
2 cinnamon sticks
500 g (18 oz) sugar
powdered cinnamon

Bring the milk to the boil in two or more saucepans. Let it cool.

Put the butter in a very large saucepan (not aluminium) over a gentle heat. When it starts to soften, brush the butter up the sides, then add the boiled cooled milk, rice, salt and cinnamon sticks. Bring to the boil and then lower the heat and cook gently, stirring frequently with a wooden spoon until it is done – about 2 hours.

Just before your rice is ready, stir in the sugar. Leave the pudding to rest for about 10 minutes before serving sprinkled with cinnamon. Well worth the time and trouble!

ARROZ CON LECHE/RICE PUDDING

143

LECHE FRITA/FRIED MILK

HIGOS Y DATILES EN VINO BLANCO
Figs and Dates in White Wine
Andalusia

This is a delicious pudding which you can experiment with by adding more dried fruits and using a sweeter wine, such as Malaga or sweet sherry, in which case you naturally use less sugar. I use less sugar and sometimes add honey.

Serves 4

1 bottle white wine
50 ml (2 fl. oz) eau de vie
zest and juice of 2 lemons
250 g (9 oz) sugar
1 cinnamon stick
5 or 6 cloves
250 g (9 oz) dried figs
250 g (9 oz) dates, stoned
single cream for serving

Put the wine, eau de vie, lemon zest and juice, sugar, cinnamon and cloves into an enamel pan. Bring to the boil, reduce the heat slightly and allow to reduce by about a third.

Add the figs and cook for about 5 minutes, then add the dates and cook for another 5 minutes. Allow to cool.

Serve chilled in individual glasses or bowls and either pour over the cream or serve separately.

LECHE FRITA
Fried Milk
Castile

This may not sound very appetizing, but it is amazing what you can do with milk and a few other ingredients.

Serves 6

100 g (4 oz) sugar
90 g (3½ oz) cornflour
500 ml (18 fl. oz) milk
a slice or two of orange and lemon peel
1 cinnamon stick
plain flour for dusting
1–2 eggs, beaten
oil for frying

Put the sugar and cornflour into a bowl with a little of the milk and stir until smooth. Heat the rest of the milk in a thick saucepan with the orange and lemon peel and the cinnamon stick. When it boils turn down the heat and gradually add the cornflour, stirring all the time with a wooden spoon until you have a thickish mixture. This should take about 3 minutes. Pour into a square or rectangular dish. The mixture should be about 2.5 cm (1 in) thick. Leave to get cold.

Cut the set mixture into squares. Dip in flour and then the beaten egg. Fry in hot oil and eat immediately. You can sprinkle with sugar and powdered cinnamon if you are a cinnamon fan like I am.

Leche frita reheats very well in a microwave oven.

GRATINADO DE FRUTAS/FRUIT GRATIN

GRATINADO DE FRUTAS
Fruit Gratin
Catalonia

This recipe was given to me when I visited the Hotel Bosch about five years ago. You can use whatever fruit is in season, but a combination of wild strawberries, raspberries and blackberries not only tastes good but looks most attractive. Keep the berries whole as otherwise they go mushy and spoil the look of the dish.

Use the combination of fruit you prefer and arrange in individual ovenproof dishes or in a larger dish. This is then covered with the cream below and placed under a hot grill for a few seconds. This cream can be prepared in advance and reheated.

Serves 8

1 kg (2¼ lb) fruit at most, prepared

CREAM
8 egg yolks
250 g (9 oz) sugar
750 ml (1¼ pints) single cream
15 ml (1 tbsp) eau de vie de framboise or
Kirsch

Beat the egg yolks with the sugar. Heat the cream in a saucepan to boiling point and stir into the egg and sugar mixture. Return it all to the saucepan you've heated the cream in and stir until it boils. Flavour with eau de vie de framboise or Kirsch, depending on the fruit you are using. Pour the cream over the fruit and place under the grill for a few seconds.

LANDSCAPE OF LA MANCHA.

PERAS EN VINO TINTO
Pears in Red Wine
Madrid

The best pears for this dish are the large, fat ones with yellowy skins. If you like things very sweet, add more sugar and honey.

Serves 4

> *500 ml (18 fl. oz) red wine*
> *a piece of lemon or orange peel*
> *30 ml (2 tbsp) brown sugar*
> *30 ml (2 tbsp) honey*
> *4 large pears*

Put the red wine in a saucepan with the peel, sugar and honey and bring to the boil. Lower the heat slightly and allow to cook while you peel the pears (leaving the stalks on if they have them). Stand the pears in the wine, cover and simmer until done – about 15 minutes. Baste them occasionally with the wine.

Put the pears into a serving dish, pour the wine over and leave to get cold. If you have peeled the pears very quickly then you may need to reduce the sauce a little more by boiling it longer but beware, I once made caramelised pears by mistake!

PERAS EN VINO TINTO/PEARS IN RED WINE

TORRIJAS
Sweet Bread
Nationwide

In Spain they sell special spongy bread to make *torrijas* which are traditionally eaten at Easter. However they can be made with any slightly stale bread that has plenty of crumbs. Instead of soaking them in milk you can also soak them in red wine. Honey makes an excellent alternative to the sugar and cinnamon that is usually sprinkled on before serving.

Serves at least 6

1 loaf of spongy or soft white bread,
preferably round in shape
110 g (4¼ oz) sugar (use more or less
depending on how sweet you like things)
1 litre (1¾ pints) milk
6 eggs
olive oil for frying
250 g (9 oz) sugar for dusting
100 g (4 oz) powdered cinnamon

Cut the bread into slices about 2.5 cm (1 in) thick. Mix the sugar into the milk and dip the slices of bread into it. Leave the bread until it is well soaked, turning as much as necessary. Next put the slices on a rack or in a colander so that any surplus liquid drains away.

Beat the eggs well and coat the *torrijas* on all sides. Heat the oil, which shouldn't be excessively hot, and fry them until they are golden on all sides. Remove, drain and sprinkle with the sugar and cinnamon and serve immediately. *Torrijas* can be eaten hot or cold, but I think they are much better freshly made.

THE LATE MEDIEVAL CLOISTERS OF CARMEN DE PERELADA CHURCH, CATALONIA.

TORRIJAS/SWEET BREAD

ROSQUILLAS
Aniseed Rings
Nationwide

There are hundreds of different varieties of *ros-quillas* made all over Spain. Sometimes they are made with lard, sometimes with oil. They can be baked in the oven or fried. These crisp biscuity rings are usually flavoured with aniseed.

Makes about 30

> 250 g (9 oz) flour
> 150 g (5 oz) sugar
> 2 egg yolks
> 50 ml (2 fl. oz) olive oil
> 200 ml (7 fl. oz) milk
> 10 ml (2 tsp) aniseeds
> oil for frying
> sugar for dusting

ROSQUILLAS/ANISEED RINGS

Sieve the flour into a bowl, and add the sugar. Beat the egg yolks and mix into the flour mixture. Then add the oil and *gradually* stir in the milk. When the mixture starts to form a dough, use your hands: the dough should not stick to your hands, so add more or less milk accordingly.

When it is the right consistency flatten it and add the aniseeds (or anise powder). Cut off strips about 2 cm (¾ in) wide and 10–12 cm (4–4½ in) long. Roll each one in your hands and twist into a round with a hole in the centre. Heat the oil nice and hot and fry until golden. Take out, drain and dip in sugar. *Rosquillas* keep well in a tin. They go well with a fruit sweet.

(*OVERLEAF*) THE RIO EBRO IN RIOJA.

DULCE DE MEMBRILLO
Quince Sweet
Nationwide

Quinces are eaten a lot in Spain, and a popular pudding is quince sweet and cheese, the cheese being either a mild Manchego or some other fairly plain cheese such as the Santander and Mahon varieties. You can buy it in slabs nearly everywhere, but some of the commercial makes tend to be too sweet.

Although I have never done it, I have often read that when you are making *dulce de membrillo*, the ideal thing is to place it covered in muslin in the sun for two days – maybe it's even better like that.

Serves 6

1 kg (2¼ lb) quinces
400 ml (14 fl. oz) water
sugar

Cut and core the quinces, and put the cores and seeds to soak in 250 ml (8 fl. oz) of the water.

Put the unpeeled fruit in a saucepan with the remaining water, bring to the boil, then reduce the heat and simmer until the fruit is completely cooked and soft – about 30 minutes. Take care it doesn't burn. You can always add a little more water if necessary, but the final result should be like a purée.

Strain the water from the cores and add to the quince purée. Liquidize and then weigh the fruit and add an equal weight of sugar. Put into a heavy saucepan and mix the sugar in well. Simmer over a very low heat stirring constantly until it thickens.

Test by dropping ½ a teaspoon on to an ice cube. When it sets sufficiently so that you can remove it in one piece, it is done. Remove from the heat and beat by hand with a wooden spoon for about 5 minutes then, when it reaches the consistency of a heavy purée, spoon into a dish lined with wax paper to a thickness of about 2–3 cm (1–1¼ in).

Allow to cool for a minimum of 24 hours, then wrap in tin foil until needed.

159